THE WOBBLIES
The U.S. vs. Wm. D. Haywood, et. al.

THE WOBBLIES
The U.S. vs. Wm. D. Haywood, et. al.

STEWART BIRD
and
PETER T. ROBILOTTA

NEW YORK, N. Y.

Acknowledgements

This publication is made possible with public funds from the New York State Council on the Arts.

Assistance for graphic work on this publication has been aided by a grant from the ADCO Foundation.

Cover: Judy Janda

© 1980 by S. Bird and P. T. Robilotta

ISBN 0-918266-13-0

Smyrna Press
Box 1803–GPO, Brooklyn, NY 11202

Printed by
Athens Printing Company
461 Eighth Avenue
New York, NY 10001

TABLE OF CONTENTS

Introduction: Joyce Kornbluh VII

ACT ONE

Scene 1: Cook County Court House. Chicago, Ill.
May, 1918 3

Scene 2: Out side the Silver Nugget Saloon. Cripple Creek,
Colorado. 1903 13

Scene 3: Boise, Idaho. 1907 15

Scene 4: Cook County Court House. June, 1918 18

Scene 5: Brandt Hall. Chicago, Ill. 1905 23

Scene 6: Cook County Court House. July, 1918 25

ACT TWO

Scene 1: Boxcar in North Dakota. 1914 35

Scene 2: Lawrence, Mass. 1912 38

Scene 3: Cook County Court House. August, 1918 45

Scene 4: Cook County Court House. September, 1918 .. 51

A Note from the Playwrights on Documentary Sources 59

Notes on Playwrights 61

THE HARVEST DRIVE IS ON AGAIN!

The Industrial Pioneer

An Illustrated Labor Magazine
July, 1925   Price 20 cents

Introduction

Although more than half a century separates the events of Stewart Bird and Peter Robilotta's play *The Wobblies* from current movements for social and economic justice in the United States, the dreams and struggles of the Industrial Workers of the World are part of the militant legacy of the labor movement, the working class, and future action agendas. The deeds of the men and women of the I.W.W. have been kept alive by poets, novelists, playwrights, and many others inspired by their gallantry and courage. "Solidarity Forever," written by I.W.W. member Ralph Chaplin, has become the labor movement's anthem sung in union halls throughout the world. "Casey Jones" and "The Preacher and the Slave" by I.W.W. protest songster Joe Hill have become part of American folklore. And the slogan "bread and roses," currently used in various working class struggles, was first lettered on a picket sign during a mass demonstration of immigrant workers: "We want bread and roses, too." In 1979, the hundred anniversary of Joe Hill's birth will be commemorated in meetings at local unions and labor history societies across the country. There also will be a series of paintings and prints by Ralph Fasinella honoring the 1912 I.W.W. Lawrence textile strike and a feature length documentary film on the I.W.W. produced by Deborah Shaffer and Stewart Bird.

What makes the I.W.W. live on and what is the relationship of this play to working-class activists today? As Fred Thompson, former editor of *The Industrial Worker* and an I.W.W. historian has said, "To many of us nothing seems more relevant to this atomic age than Joe Hill's lines 'working men of all countries unite, side by side we for freedom will fight.' And our hopes still run to what can be done 'if workers take a notion and realize that, there is power in a band of working men'." Transforming the processes of work and daily life, organizing the unorganized, struggling for job control and industrial democracy, shorter work days and work weeks, higher wages, health and safety on the job, job security — issues that the Wobblies fought for in the first quarter of this century — are still major concerns for workers and union members in the 1980s The need for dynamic leadership to energize low-paid workers, women and minorities to express their collective power; the need for imaginative, broad-based organizing approaches to ignite an effective movement of workers in low-paid industries; and a recognition of the need for basic economic and social structural changes in the society are an I.W.W. legacy as well as an imperative agenda for today.

In *The Wobblies*, Bird and Robilotta have captured the realities as well as the romance of the I.W.W.—their hardships, their tough-minded humor, their songs and slogans of protest and parody, their disillusionment with and alienation from capitalist society, their militancy and solidarity in the face of repression: the whole texture of the life of working-class radicals in the first three decades of this century.

Late in 1904, leaders of the Western Federation of Miners initiated a meeting in Chicago to consider plans for a new, national revolutionary union. The six radicals who attended invited thirty prominent socialists and labor activists to another secret conference in the same city in January 1905. The January conference drafted the *Industrial Union Manifesto*, a radical analysis of economic and social relations, that spelled out labor's grievances, criticized existing craft unions for creating a skilled labor aristocracy, and recommended "... one big industrial union ... founded on the class struggle." Large numbers of the *Manifesto* were sent around the country and workers who agreed with its principles were invited to attend a convention in Chicago, beginning on June 27, 1905, to found a new revolutionary, working-class organization.

Approximately two hundred delegates from thirty-four organizations congregated for this founding convention. Socialists, anarchists, radical miners — all advocates of industrial unionism — were united in their opposition to the elitist craft union philosophy and conservative practices of the American Federation of Labor and by their desire to replace the capitalist economic system with a "cooperative commonwealth of workers." The I.W.W. delegates viewed the American economy in class terms. They believed that a class struggle was inherent in the very nature of a capitalist system and that since employers had united into great combinations of capital to maintain their supremacy in industrial, social and governmental institutions, it was necessary to organize all workers, skilled and unskilled, into industrial unions that would have the power to combat the integrated power of modern capital. Big Bill Haywood, an organizer for the Western Federation of Miners, opened the sessions, "Fellow Workers: This is the Continental Congress of the Working Class. We are here to confederate the workers of this country into a working-class movement in possession of the economic powers, the means of life, in control of the machinery of production and distribution without regard to capitalist masters."

In summary, the newly formed Industrial Workers of the World held that (1) employers and workers have diametrically conflicting interests; (2) the wage system must be replaced by an industrial society controlled by the workers themselves; (3) labor unions must be organized on industrial rather than on craft lines; (4) labor's goals must be secured by industrial rather than by political action since most workers were disenfranchised—blacks, women, immigrants and those without property in some sections of the country did not have the right to vote; and (5) a new moral and social code emphasizing the rights of human life and happiness must replace the capitalist system's emphasis on the rights of property. Most of these ideas were clearly expressed in the *Preamble* to the I.W.W. constitution, written during those days in June 1905, with its ringing words that were to be translated into many languages:

> The working class and the employing class have nothing in common. There can be no peace so long as hunger and want are found among millions of working people, and the few, who make up the employing class, have all the good things of life.
>
> Between these two classes a struggle must go on until the workers of the world organize as a class, take possession of the earth and the machinery of production, and abolish the wage system.
>
> We find that the centering of the management of industries into fewer and fewer hands makes the trade unions unable to cope with the ever growing power of the employing class. The trade unions foster a state of affairs which allows one set of workers to be pitted against another set of workers in the same industry, thereby helping defeat one another in wage wars. Moreover, the trade unions aid the employing class to mislead the workers into the belief that the working class have interests in common with their employers.
>
> These conditions can be changed and the interest of the working class upheld only by an organization formed in such a way that all its members in any one industry, or in all industries, if necessary, cease work whenever a strike or lockout is on in any department, Thereby making an injury to one an injury to all.
>
> Instead of the conservative motto, "A fair day's wage

for a fair day's work," we must inscribe on our banner the revolutionary watchword, "Abolition of the wage system."

It is the historic mission of the working class to do away with capitalism. The army of production must be organized, not only for the every-day struggle with capitalists, but also to carry on production when capitalism shall have been overthrown. By organizing industrially we are forming the structure of the new society within the shell of the old. (as amended in 1908)

Any wage earner could be a member of the new organization, regardless of his or her job, race or creed. Immigrants with paid up union cards in their native country were eligible for immediate membership. Initiation fees and dues were low; labor-management contracts were viewed as an interference with labor's only weapon—the strike, and contracts were rejected because they kept workers from declaring strikes when employers might be most vulnerable. The "social general strike" was recommended as the most effective weapon in the overthrow of industrial capitalism; militarism was condemned and membership could be denied anyone who joined the state militia or police.

As Stewart Bird and Peter Robilotta point out in their play, Haywood was one of the most colorful and forceful labor leaders in American history, articulating the need to organize the forgotten and dispossessed and stressing that industrial unions would become the basis for the socialist society of the future. As an article in the I.W.W. paper, *Solidarity*, later stated, "The I.W.W. is organizing for porkchops in the present and for a new social system."

For the next decade, the I.W.W. became a militant vehicle for class war in the United States, directing or taking part in at least one hundred and fifty strikes. These strikes were to strengthen the working-class at the expense of the employer as well as a means to weaken the capitalist system. The general strike was viewed in the broadest sense as the peaceful taking over of the means of production once the workers had been organized. It would be brought about, said Haywood and other I.W.W. organizers, by the "folded arms" of the workers. "When we strike now, we strike with our hands in our pockets. . . . We have a new kind of violence, the havoc we raise with money by laying down our tools," Haywood told a reporter in 1913 during the textile strike in Lawrence, Massachusetts.

However, although I.W.W. activists succeeded in setting up strike committees, encouraging rank and file participation and welding diverse nationality groups into a cohesive whole, I.W.W. organizers

INTRODUCTION

rarely remained after a strike to build a strong union organization. Once a strike was won, no contracts would be recognized. Only temporary "truces" could be effected on the battlefield of capital and labor. The philosophy of strikes was expressed in one of the colorful I.W.W. songs:

> Why do you make agreements that divide you when you fight,
> And let the bosses bluff you with the contract's
>   "sacred right?"
> Why stay at work when other crafts are battling with the foe;
> You must all stick together, don't you know.
>
> Tie' em up! Tie' em up! That's the way to win;
> Don't notify the bosses 'til hostilities begin;
> Don't furnish chance for gunmen, scabs and all their like;
> What you need is One Big Union and the One Big Strike!

I.W.W. members "tied up" their bosses by assorted forms of harassment on the job, often called "sabotage" or "conscientious withdrawal of efficiency"—harassment that proved to be the most controversial concept affecting the organization. The tactics of direct action evolved from the nature of working conditions of most I.W.W. members who frequently had to resort to short, decisive actions in place of long-term costly strikes. I.W.W. sabotage aimed to ". . . hit the employer in his vital spot, his heart and soul, in other words, his pocketbook." It encompassed actions that might disable machinery, slacken production, spoil a product, or reduce a company's profit by telling the truth about its merchandise. Sabotage was defined as another form of coercion, part of the internal industrial process, rather than as physical violence.

Bold rhetoric in I.W.W. literature and propaganda continued to dramatize the evils of the industrial system, and the wooden shoe and black cat symbols for sabotage appeared widely in I.W.W. prose, song and illustration. Small propaganda stickers pasted onto fences, walls of box cars, and railroad sidings and I.W.W. posters and cartoons showed a haunched black cat baring its claws, and the words "sab cat," "kitten," "fix the job," were used to suggest or to threaten striking on the job, direct action, and workers' power.

While it would be difficult, at this time, to document whether or not I.W.W. members practiced lawlessness and violence, many researchers over the years have concluded that such reports were exaggerated and that there is no evidence that the members engaged in widespread destructive sabotage. However, bold free speech fights and inflammatory propaganda brought the impact of the organization to the doorstep of many communities across the country and its radical theories and militant strikes resulted in legal and illegal attempts to repress the organization.

The most important strikes that the I.W.W. directed or took part in include the Goldfield, Nevada, miners' strike of 1906-1907; the Lawrence, Massachusetts, textile workers' strike of 1912; the Paterson, New Jersey, silk workers strike of 1913; and the iron workers' strike on the Masabi Range in Minnesota in 1916. The I.W.W.'s most important units were made up of workers in lumbering, construction, agriculture, dock work and marine transport, but it was also successful for periods of time in eastern textile towns, in the oil fields of Oklahoma and in Colorado's coal mines. Although the organization never had more than about 100,000 members at the peak of its activities, it shook the nation with an impact disproportionate to its size.

Three stars on the I.W.W. banner, printed on all forms of its propaganda, were labeled "education," "organization," "emancipation." Education was carried on through propaganda leagues, industrial education clubs, constant leafleting, and widespread circulation of the I.W.W. newspapers, *Solidarity* and *The Industrial Worker*, both started around 1909. By the end of 1912, foreign-language branches of the I.W.W. were publishing newspapers in French, Italian, Spanish, Portuguese, Yiddish, Russian, Polish, Slavic, Lithuanian, Hungarian, Swedish and Japanese. Most I.W.W. halls included libraries of I.W.W. literature and books by Karl Marx, Herbert Spencer, Charles Darwin, Voltaire, Jack London, Thomas Paine, government publications and a wide range of material on economics and social sciences. Unemployed I.W.W. members frequently spent time in public libraries reading philosophy, economics and science. Jailed during free speech fights or organizing campaigns and strikes, members would set up their own circulating prison libraries, publish handwritten I.W.W. newspapers and occasionally stage prison 'entertainments,' which might include book reviews, debates, lectures and educational skits.

Some of the best educational material published by the I.W.W. was included in 'the little red songbook'. As one I.W.W. organizer wrote in 1912, "There are thirty-eight songs in the I.W.W. songbook and out of that number twenty-four are educational and I can truthfully say that every one of them is almost a lecture in itself." The songbook was started by the Spokane branch of the I.W.W. about 1909 and was given the provocative subtitle, "songs to fan the flames of discontent." In the more than thirty-five editions of the songbook from 1909 to the present there have been some 180 songs. Folklorist John Greenway has called the I.W.W. songbook '... the first great collection of labor songs ever assembled for utilitarian purposes.' Over the years the contents of the little red song book dramatized the class-conscious philosophy of the I.W.W. and reflected the spirit, humor and experiences of migratory and seasonal workers. Although the I.W.W.'s most talented and prolific songwriter was Joe Hill, other contributors included Richard Brazier, Ralph Chaplin, Covington Hall, and Laura Payne Emerson. I.W.W. songs were sung on picket lines, in hobo jungles, at mass meetings, during free speech demonstrations—wherever members gathered to agitate for a new world built "from the ashes of the old."

The I.W.W. pioneered in the use of free speech fights—not to defend a constitutional principle or to attract publicity but to recruit members in the 'slave market' sections of cities where unemployed workers gathered between jobs. From 1907 to 1917, the Wobblies conducted some thirty struggles to establish the right to speak on street corners to workers about job conditions and about the economic conditions in the United States during those years, such as rising prices, stationary wages, a series of depressions, widespread unemployment, which after the financial panic of 1908 was close to 36 percent in all trades, corporation mergers and rapidly changing technology. Millions of unemployed drifted in search of work from one town to another, most making their way on freight cars and finding temporary jobs harvesting crops, sawing lumber, cutting ice, building roads, laying railroad ties. In 1908, for example, although a minimum of $800 a year was necessary to support a family, half the adult fathers earned under $600 and a quarter earned under $400 a year.

Each of the free speech fights followed a similar pattern. I.W.W. organizers would issue a call through handbills and through the I.W.W. press for "foot loose rebels" to come to a certain town where a campaign would be underway. In response, hundreds of members and sympathizers would arrive by box car, mount streetcorner soapboxes, talk about the exploitation of workers, and be thrown into jails. Soon the crowded prisons, clogged municipal court machinery, and the high costs of paying for extra police would lead the town fathers to rescind the municipal ordinance against street organizing and to release the jailed radicals.

The boldness and intransigence of the I.W.W. rebels frequently turned the free speech fights into bitter, bloody battles. As the San Diego *Tribune* editorialized about the Wobblies during a 1912 free speech campaign in that city, "Hanging is none too good for them."

They would be much better dead for they are absolutely useless in the human economy. They are the waste material of creation and should be drained off into the sewer of oblivion, there to rot in cold obstruction like any other excrement." The *Tribune* also called for the shooting or hanging of all I.W.W. members jailed for free speech campaigning, which, it claimed "... would end the trouble in an hour." Vigilante committees, frequently in collusion with police and local officials, would seize I.W.W. prisoners on their release from jail, load them into cars, drive to the edge of town where they would be beaten, pistol whipped, at times tarred and feathered or shot. In 1912, in response to demands from several California organizations to investigate vigilante brutality against I.W.W. free speech campaigners, Governor Hiram Johnson appointed a fact-finding commission. The investigation report emphasized the passive resistance of the I.W.W. campaigners and the lack of violence or drunkeness among I.W.W. members. It also scored the police for "needless brutality" and substantiated the reports of beatings by "... so-called vigilantes ... part of whom were police officers, part constables, and part private citizens." None of the vigilantes, however, was ever apprehended or tried.

Despite their failure to organize permanent, stable local unions, the organizing campaigns, the strikes and the free speech fights made a profound impression on the public and the rest of the labor movement by dramatizing the plight of the forgotten workers and communicating the spirit of their rebellion. Following the 1912 Lawrence, Massachusetts textile strike, literary critic Kenneth McGowan wrote in *Forum:*

> Whatever its future, the I.W.W. has accomplished one tremendously big thing, a thing that sweeps away all twaddle over red flags and violence and sabotage, and that is the individual awakening of "illiterates' and 'scum' to an original, personal conception of society and the realization of the dignity and rights of their part in it. They have learned more than class consciousness; they have learned consciousness of self.

Preceding and during World War I, the I.W.W. took an antimilitarist stand, opposed the entrance of the United States into the war, and continued to lead strikes in contrast to the no-strike pledge of the American Federation of Labor. Since the 1905 founding of the organization, members had opposed war because, as I.W.W. soapboxer J. P. Thompson frequently stated, "In a broad sense,

INTRODUCTION

there is no such thing as a foreigner. We are all native-born members of this planet and for members of it to be divided into groups or units and taught that each nation is better than others leads to clashes and world war. We ought to have in the place of national patriotism—the idea that one people is better than another—a broader concept—that of international solidarity."

As early as 1914, the I.W.W. declared itself officially opposed to World War I in a convention resolution that stated, "We as members of the industrial army will refuse to fight for any purpose except the realization of industrial freedom." I.W.W. writers and speakers lambasted the European conflict as an object lesson in capitalist folly in which workers were being sent into slaughter to line the pockets of the owners of industry. I.W.W. leaders maintained that I.W.W. strikes of this period were not attempts to sabotage the war effort, but were industrial disputes to improve conditions for workers in agriculture, lumbering and mining. A president's mediation commission, investigating the I.W.W.-led strikes in Arizona, supported this view. Although the strikes were denounced by many companies as pro-German and seditious, the commission reported that "... they appeared to be nothing more than the normal results of the increased cost of living and the speeding up processes to which the mine management had been tempted by the abnormally high market price of copper."

However, frightened at the prospects of labor shortages at a time when there was a heightened demand for their products, employers vented their fury on dissenters who, they claimed, were threatening national security and the capitalist system. In Tulsa, Oklahoma, the *Daily World* editorialized, "The first step in the whipping of Germany is to strangle the I.W.W.'s. Kill them, just as you would kill any other kind of snake. Don't scotch them; kill' em dead. It's no time to waste money on trials and continuances and things like that. All that is necessary is the evidence and a firing squad." The charges that the Wobblies were German agents or that their strikes were supported by Kaiser gold were widespread but were never verified by the slightest evidence. In fact, newspaper reporter Robert Breure who interviewed Northwest lumber operators about the I.W.W. wrote that one employer told him, "In war—and a strike is war—anything is fair.... Of course, we have taken advantage of the general prejudice against them as an unpatriotic organization to beat their strike." Although the organization remained anti-military after the United States entered the war, it neither officially opposed the draft nor staged any anti-war strikes.

Little effort went into protecting I.W.W. members from government and community hysteria. Army troups and community vigilante groups raided I.W.W. halls and members' homes across the country, dispersed outdoor gatherings, disrupted meetings and jailed members. In 1918 and 1919, 184 I.W.W. members were tried by the federal government in Chicago, Sacramento and Wichita, on charges of interfering with the war effort and advocating resistance to the Selective Service Act. Defendants were charged with conspiring to obstruct the war effort through sabotaging industry and destroying property, by propagandizing against the war and resisting the draft. The I.W.W. cases involved the largest number of persons convicted of opposing World War I. The jury in the Chicago trial, which had lasted five months, took less than an hour to find 100 of the defendants guilty. Many of the convicted were sentenced to twenty years in prison. In separate trials in Sacramento, California, and Wichita, Kansas, an additional sixty-nine I.W.W. members were imprisoned, although in none of the three trials was a single act cited to justify the charges that the I.W.W. was a "vicious, treasonable conspiracy to oppose by force the execution of the laws of the United States and to obstruct the prosecution of the war."

The post-war years were marked by further indictments of I.W.W. members under the criminal syndicalism statutes of many states, and considerable community hostility to radicalism in all forms, which led to continued repression of the organization. Legal defense and amnesty campaigns sapped the organization's strength for a number of years. In addition, controversy racked the membership over what terms the jailed members should accept for amnesty. Internal organizational discord also focused around relations with the American Communist Party, organized in 1919. The I.W.W. had been sympathetic to the Bolshevik Revolution and in 1920, Moscow wooed the I.W.W. to join the Communist International, praising the "... long and heroic service of the I.W.W. in the class war." Some of the leaders and activists such as Bill Haywood, Elizabeth Gurley Flynn, George Hardy and Charles Ashleigh were attracted to Soviet communism. Indeed, Haywood skipped bail, as the play notes, and fled to the Soviet Union, where he died in 1928. The majority of I.W.W. members, however, held to the belief in the gradual acquisition of control of industry by economic action on the job. This was in contrast to the Communist Party position which accepted industrial unionism but insisted that it is necessary to overthrow the capitalist state and organize a dictatorship of the proletariat in order to build a new society.

Following World War I, the I.W.W. became the victim of changing American industrial technology, changes that it had anticipated since its inception in 1905 and against which it continued to rebel. The expanding use of farm machinery threw thousands of migrant agricultural workers out of jobs. The "auto tramp" replaced the hobo "bindle stiff" as whole families traveled by jalopy from one town to another in search of work, and "homeguards" instead of single transient workers were hired by the logging industry. Ruthless employer suppression of all attempts of union organization during the 'open shop' campaigns of the 1920's and fundamental changes in the economy and the workforce led to further losses in membership. Many of the prisoners were not released from jails until the middle or late 1920s. Despite these problems, the I.W.W. carried on its organizing activities for the next several decades, contributing its philosophy of industrial unionism and laying the groundwork for the mass organization of unskilled, and semi-skilled workers in the C.I.O. and many A.F.L. unions of the thirties and forties.

During the Depression, the I.W.W. joined with organizations of unemployed workers to set up Unemployed Unions to provide housing and food for the jobless. Throughout 1932 and 1933, I.W.W. organization and agitation in Detroit added impetus to the growing unrest of auto workers suffering from layoffs, wage cuts and the tensions of speed-up in the auto plants. Soapboxing, leafleting, a weekly radio program and weekend socials in the Detroit I.W.W. hall provided the growth of a skeleton organization in some of the large auto plants, which helped spur quickie strikes in the Briggs, Hudson and Murray Body auto plants. Some of the I.W.W. organizers moved on to Cleveland, where, during the next few years, they organized members in several foundries and metal shops. Shops organized in 1934, such as the American Stove Company, were still in the I.W.W. in 1950, the longest record of collective bargaining in the organization's history.

During World War II, spurts of I.W.W. activity carried on in western mining camps and along the waterfronts led *Business Week* to comment in January 1945, "The I.W.W. shows signs of life. In the metal shops of Cleveland, on the waterfront of San Diego, New Orleans and New York the dead past is stirring and men are carrying red cards. "However, despite its opposition to the Communist Party, the organization was placed on Attorney General Tom Clark's list of subversive organizations. Soon afterwards, the U.S. Treasury Department ruled that it was subject to a corporate income tax and another blow came when the I.W.W. leaders on principle refused to sign the noncommunist affidavit required by the 1947 Taft-Hartley Act, and in the process lost the Cleveland local.

The I.W.W. persists to the present day, its newspaper and publications as lively and provocative as in the past. Recently, it donated its archives to the Walter Reuther Labor Archives at Wayne State University in Detroit at a meeting commemorating the fiftieth anniversary of Joe Hill's death. Small local unions exist in several areas and in recent years, there has been a resurgent interest in I.W.W. philosophy and organization. I.W.W. strike techniques—the sitdowns in Schenectady and Detroit, the chain picketing in Lawrence, the car caravans in Colorado—once considered revolutionary, became the practices of later A.F.L. and C.I.O. unions. I.W.W. free speech fights, trials and persecutions by vigilante groups aroused liberals across the country to the need for defense organizations to protect the rights of dissenters. I.W.W. fights for better conditions in logging camp bunkhouses and on farms focused attention on the problems of migratory agricultural workers, and their agitation in jails against notorious prison abuses eventually helped bring about more humane prison conditions. Recent scholarly work on the Wobblies included Melvin Dubofsky's *We Shall Be All*, Patrick Renshaw's *The Wobblies*, Philip Foner's *The Industrial Workers of the World 1905-1917*, William Preston's *Aliens and Dissenters*, Joseph Conlin's *Bread and Roses*, Gibbs Smith's *Joe Hill*, and Fred Thompson's *The I.W.W., Its First Seventy Years*. Numerous articles on the organization have appeared in *Labor History*, and in regional labor history, industrial relations and folklore journals. Recent scholarly books on the I.W.W.'s role in American labor history have appeared in Sweden, Australia, Italy and Japan.

If I.W.W. songwriter Joe Hill were to return to earth today, he probably would still be writing songs about "Pie in the Sky." Despite the Square Deals, the New Freedoms, the New Deals, the New Frontier, the War on Poverty and the Great Society, the goal of rendering people secure from the dread of war and the fear of want in a democratic society has not been realized. The spirit of the rebels in the Industrial Workers of the World lives on not only in folklore, but in the contributions those militants made to the American labor movement. Plays such as *The Wobblies* which hopefully will be performed by community groups throughout the country help to keep alive their dreams and to actualize Joe Hill's message, "Don't mourn: organize."

—Joyce L. Kornbluh

ACT ONE

SCENE ONE

(A scrim covers the stage at the apron. As the house lights go down a slide show is projected on the scrim. The sound track is synchronized with the slides. The slides begin with working conditions and union organizing 1900-1918. The music is ragtime; it changes to George M. Cohan and we see recruiting posters, soldiers marching, troop ships and scenes of the war in Europe. The music changes to IWW songs and we see pictures of workers, lumberjacks, farm hands, children in textile mills, organizers, demonstrators, picket lines, police, troops and arrests. Finally we see newspaper headlines; the following voice over is heard on the sound track. The slides continue of jail scenes, Chicago 1918, and headlines about the trial. The last slide is a rendering of the set.)

JAILER: What's your name?
IWW VOICE 1: Sam Scarlet.
JAILER: What's your religion?
IWW VOICE 1: The IWW.
JAILER: That ain't no religion.
IWW VOICE 1: It's the only one I got.
JAILER: Who's your next of kin?
IWW VOICE 2: Don't have any.
JAILER: Well, who's your best friend?
IWW VOICE 2: Big Bill Haywood.
JAILER: He's in here with you. He can't help you.
IWW VOICE 2: He's still my best friend.
JAILER: What's your nationality?
IWW VOICE 1: None.
JAILER: Well, what country are you a citizen of?
IWW VOICE 1: I'm a citizen of industry.
JAILER: Where is your home?
IWW VOICE 2: Cook County Jail.
JAILER: Before that?
IWW VOICE 2: County Jail, Cleveland, Ohio.

JAILER: And before that?
IWW VOICE 2: City Jail, Akron, Ohio.
JAILER: Look, are you a citizen?
IWW VOICE 2: No, I'm an Industrial Worker of the World.

(We hear a jail door slam shut. The slide on the scrim fades and the lights come up behind the scrim. We see Nebeker and Vanderveer flanking a prospective juror. The juror does not answer but turns to each attorney as he speaks.)

VANDERVEER: Do you believe in slavery? That is, do you believe in chattel slavery, where the boss owns the worker, body and soul?
NEBEKER: Do you believe in the wage system and in the social system as it is now organized?
VANDERVEER: Do you agree that most prostitution is caused because women in industry do not get living wages? . . . Do you recognize the right of the people to rebel against this injustice?
NEBEKER: Have you any sympathy with any organization that seeks to overthrow the institutions of this country or to violate its laws?
VANDERVEER: Do you believe in the right of the people to govern themselves and to have a voice in this government?
NEBEKER: Do you believe that free speech gives anyone the right to advocate the breaking of the law?
VANDERVEER: Do you believe that industry should make the laws for people to live by?
NEBEKER: Were you in favor of the declaration of war against the Imperial German Government?
VANDERVEER: Well, were you?

(The JUROR stares first at one lawyer and then at the other, afraid to give any response.)

NEBEKER: I accept him.
VANDERVEER: So do I.

(Judge Landis who has been watching the proceedings from his perch on the bench bangs his gavel. He is an elderly man with a lot of enthusiasm. He is very mobile, frequently moving around the courtroom, sitting with the prosecutor, the defense and the jury. He removes his robes on Nebeker's next line and we see him in suspenders and shirt sleeves during the rest of the trial. The scrim opens.)

LANDIS: The Federal District Court of the First District, Chicago, Illinois, this day April First, 1918 is now in session. The case of the United States vs. William D. Haywood, *et al.* Having heard the reading of the charges ... Mr. Nebeker? ... proceed.

NEBEKER: May it please the court, gentlemen of the jury, this is not a flippant trial, this is not a minor trial, this is not the trial of a patriotic labor union, for the IWW can in no way be considered a labor union. It is in fact a criminal conspiracy which has obstructed the prosecution of the war against Imperial Germany. We shall prove that the IWW ...

LANDIS: Mr. Nebeker, could you speak up please?

NEBEKER: WE SHALL PROVE that the IWW is guilty of these things, gentlemen of the jury. Beyond the shadow of a doubt ... Now on the first charge let me enumerate ...

(Nebeker continues in pantomime; the narrator enters. He is a middle-aged reporter; whenever he enters the set action continues in pantomime and he speaks to the audience.)

NARRATOR: Beyond the shadow of a doubt, you know it's funny what you remember and what you forget. Now I usually can't remember dates for nothing, anything to do with numbers, but I can remember every one of Walter Johnson's 56 consecutive scoreless innings in 1913 and Hippo Vaughn's earned run average for 1917, an incredible 1.74; you all remember Hippo, he was possibly the greatest and certainly the biggest pitcher in baseball. I watched him pitch for the Cubs against Boston, he had a screwball that looked like a figure eight.

But ask me today's date or when Arch Duke Ferdinand was assassinated or even why, I couldn't tell ya. Now for me that's a liability, I'm a reporter, cover sports and politics. Sports are a lot more exciting.... except when the Wobblies were involved; they were like a fine baseball team, a lot of spirit, a lot of hussle, a lot of guts.

... and everybody remembers Ty Cobb, they can tell you all his statistics ... there are people who can tell you his batting average for 1911 ... 420 ... or how many bases he stole in 1915 ... 96 ... but who remembers that one-eyed giant over there, Bill Haywood, to me he was just as great; it's a shame he didn't go into baseball, besides knocking the cover off the ball, there would have been one hell of a players' union.

... It's a good thing this trial didn't overlap the World Series, 'cause Judge Landis had a private box right behind first base, Wrigley Field, and he would have adjourned the trial for sure. There he sits, a small man on a huge bench, a wasted man with untidy hair, the face of Andrew Jackson, three years dead. Judge Kenesaw Mountain Landis, named for a great Civil War battle. It was Landis who fined Standard Oil $39,000,000 for taking kick-backs from the railroads. Of course, none of it was ever paid. He conducted this trial, like most of his trials, with the formality of a bar-room brawl.

Yeah! It's funny what you remember. I'll never forget the day this trial started, One April 1918, April Fools' Day; you should have seen that court room, I doubt if there's ever been a sight like it. One hundred and one men, lumberjacks, harvest hands, miners, poets, and they all believe the wealth of the land belongs to him who creates it and that's what got them in trouble. It was like an all-star team of radicals. It was more like a convention that a trial; half the time, I didn't know who was trying who.

(Nebeker picks up at end of speech and is addressing the jury. Narrator exits.)

NEBEKER: ... and so, gentlemen of the jury, having proven these things to you, I shall expect, I shall demand a verdict of guilty on each and every charge for each and every defendant, for we are locked in a Great War in Europe and to allow this kind of treason at home shall surely prove to our grave disadvantage in the trenches of France. I thank you.

LANDIS: Thank you, counselor ... Mr. Vanderveer? ... Does the defense wish to present an opening argument now?

VANDERVEER: Yes, we do, thank you, Your Honor. Let me open by saying that this case is unusual. It is supposed to be a case against William Dudley Haywood and a great number of other men that you have probably never heard of by name ... 100 other men, to be exact. Yet, in reality, this is not so. In reality, it is the purpose of the prosecution to destroy the union with which these men are connected. In simple terms, let me tell you what the defendants are charged with: conspiring to hamper the war effort ... conspiring ... I'm curious to see how our esteemed prosecutor will prove this, since most of these men had not even met prior to their arrest. The prosecutor will also tell you the IWW is conspiring to destroy our government, but that is not so either. I want you to keep your mind on this one point, on the question of whether or not the purpose of this organization is to destroy the government or merely to change an industrial system which ought to be independent of our government... which ought to be under the control of the workers. We now live in what is considered the wealthiest nation in the world. But it is a nation in which 2% of the people own over ⅔ of all its wealth... A nation in which 8 out of 10 workers are utterly unable to support their families and educate their children on a plane of civic decency. Why is this, you might ask? Might it be because the monopolies and trusts are able to hoard huge profits for themselves and yet not pay a living wage?

NEBEKER: I object, Your Honor. General industrial conditions are not involved in this case at all. Whatever those conditions are, they are based upon the law.

LANDIS: Overruled. Continue, Mr. Vanderveer.

VANDERVEER: Thank you, Your Honor... A nation in which one man, reputed to be worth a billion dollars, owns more of the wealth of this country than two and one-half million of the poorer families...

NEBEKER: I object. How can the court allow counsel to defame one of the leading citizens of our country?

LANDIS: Sustained. Please stick to the issue, counselor.

VANDEVEER: Of course... I'll close by answering the charge that I'm certain the prosecution will return to again and again, in many guises. The charge that the IWW is not patriotic. Now if patriotism means to wave flags from the housetops and then profiteer, if patriotism means that one must believe in war as the best way of settling things... that the wholesale slaughter of people is right... then the IWW is unpatriotic. But if patriotism is the belief in the people of the nation and the hope for their betterment, and the willingness of the people to work and fight and die for that betterment, then the IWW is patriotic without peer. These men are guilty of nothing more than belonging to a labor union, a labor union that recognizes that this war is not being fought to keep the world safe for democracy but merely to expand industrial markets; men are dying right now, will continue to die simply to make the rich, richer... the IWW believes that if all workers recognized that, they would refuse to fight and there could be no war. Thank you.

LANDIS: Prepare to call your first witness, Mr. Vanderveer.

(Vanderveer moves to the defense table.)

HAYWOOD: Nice going, Van.
DORAN: Yah! Great...
VANDERVEER: Well, it's a start.

DORAN: ... towards what? When you start somewhere you got to be going somewhere.
HAYWOOD: What the hell are you talking about now?
DORAN: I'm talking about a silent defense, no talking, not a word... let's at least try and keep our self-respect.
HAYWOOD: Doran, you couldn't keep your mouth shut for 5 minutes.
DORAN: If you participate in it, you're a party to it, right?
VANDERVEER: Don't worry, Red, just stick to the defense strategy.
DORAN: Look, I'm tired of this defense strategy crap; you got me to cut my hair, shave off my beard; I'm sitting here in somebody else's suit...
HAYWOOD: What's a matter, you don't like the cut, maybe we could take it in a little... *(indicating around Red's neck)*.
DORAN: What a joke... you know this whole thing is being run from Washington.
HAYWOOD: Would you rather have it run from Wall Street?
DORAN: That's one hell of a choice.
VANDERVEER: Listen, you guys, we got no problems, why half the gallery is filled with my creditors, waiting for me to win this case so they can get paid.
DORAN: I hope you know where the back door is... sap.

(Vanderveer shakes his head and walks to the exhibits. Landis now in shirt sleeves and suspenders comes over to the defense table.)

LANDIS: How you guys doin'?

(Doran is like stone, continues reading his paper.)

HAYWOOD: Hi, ya Judge, about this circus parade and the grub....
LANDIS: *(In a congenial helpful manner)*. Listen William, I'm gonna cut that out, there's no need for you fellows to be marched through the streets in shackles just to get lunch. We don't need to put on a show for those lunatics out there. From now on you eat at the court house. And if there are any complaints about the food or anything else, just tell Vanderveer and I will personally take care of it.
HAYWOOD: That's mighty considerate, Judge.

LANDIS: Don't mention it. (*Looking at Doran*) Who's throwing for Boston today? DOORen.

(Doran hands Landis the paper.)

DORAN: DoorANN, Judge, it's DoorANN. (*To Haywood*) Where are you and your friend lunching today, Bill?
HAYWOOD: Aw! Get off my back, DOORen.

(Vanderveer returns to table.)

VANDERVEER: Well, you ready Bill? You're on next.

(Haywood gives him a thumbs up sign but doesn't look that good.)

VANDERVEER: What's a matter, Bill? Don't tell me Red's getting to you?
HAYWOOD: Well, if you'd been in a cell with him for eight months... He's got his head stuck in the sand.
DORAN: You're the ostrich, sap.... I know a necktie party when I see one.
HAYWOOD: The problem with you, Doran, is that you can only look at things one way... right now, it's the wrong way....
VANDERVEER: I call William D. Haywood, for the defense.

(Haywood moves to the stand.)

DORAN: Wrong way for who, you or us?

(Haywood hesitates but continues to the witness chair. Haywood is sworn in and takes the stand.)

VANDERVEER: Your name is William D. Haywood?
HAYWOOD: Yes, Sir.
VANDERVEER: How old are you?
HAYWOOD: Forty-nine.
VANDERVEER: You are now General Secretary of the Industrial Workers of the World?
HAYWOOD: Yes, Sir.
VANDERVEER: How long have you occupied that position?
HAYWOOD: Three years.
VANDERVEER: What line of work have you followed, Mr. Haywood?
HAYWOOD: Mining, principally.

VANDERVEER: At what age did you start out in the world to make your own living?
HAYWOOD: You mean when I first began working?
VANDERVEER: Yes.
HAYWOOD: Well, I was still living at home then. I was a little less than nine years old.
LANDIS: How old were you, Mr. Haywood?
HAYWOOD: Nine years old.
LANDIS: Excuse me, what is your background, I mean what did your father do for a living?
HAYWOOD: He was a pony express rider, but he died when I was very young.

(Landis motions to Vanderveer to continue.)

VANDERVEER: What kind of work did you do then, when you were nine years old?
HAYWOOD: I was helping my step-father in the mine.
VANDERVEER: In what way?
HAYWOOD: Twisting drill, carrying steel and water, blowing the bellows.
LANDIS: Excuse me again, how did you lose that eye, William? I'm curious about that.
HAYWOOD: I was working at Couer d'Alene, copper mine, 12 hour night shift. We were going down in the cage to the shaft house floor, the cable pulled loose and dropped us forty feet down the shaft, a pick went through the eye. But I was lucky, two men died. We found out later the company had neglected the usual precautions and the hoist engine brakes were out of order.
LANDIS: Thank you, William, go ahead.
VANDERVEER: Where was I, Bill?
HAYWOOD: You were asking me where I worked when I was nine.
VANDERVEER: Oh, yes... what other work did you do as a young man?
HAYWOOD: When I was eleven, I was bound out to work on a farm. My main job was driving a yoke of oxen. I was only a kid, I guess I wasn't going fast enough. The farmer picked up a bull whip and struck me without saying a word. I ran straight to the house, gathered my belongings, and started for home. I guess you could call that my first strike.
VANDERVEER: When did you first get involved with unions?
HAYWOOD: When I first went to work in the mines, on my own, I

met the oldest miner in the camp; he was a member of the Knights of Labor. His name was ... uh. ...

DORAN: Pat Reynolds. ...

HAYWOOD: Yeah, Pat Reynolds, well he pointed out that the man eating with us, the boss, was not the real owner of the mine. The owners lived in California while the men who did all the work and made the mines of value were there in the wilderness of Nevada. I soon learned that it was necessary for working men to organize for mutual protection and that's what I have been doing ever since.

VANDERVEER: What was the first union you joined?

HAYWOOD: The Western Federation of Miners.

VANDERVEER: While you were a member of the Western Federation of Miners, did you go through any strikes in the mining industry?

HAYWOOD: While I was on the executive board, there were a number of strikes.

(Narrator enters.)

NARRATOR: You can say that again, the Western Federation of Miners, more like a war. Damn, they were my first big assignment out of New York City. I got off a stage coach in Cripple Creek, Colorado ... started asking questions and wound up in the can ... that's where I first met Big Bill, we hit it off right away ... he sort of broke me in you might say ... I'd never seen a strike, close up, before. I always figured it was picket lines and negotiation ... but the Western Federation set me straight about that ... these guys were at war and I do mean war and everybody that was invited came, including the militia. ...

The militia, if you all think of the militia as a peace-keeping organization, you don't know nothin' about Colorado in 1903. No sir ... the militia was busy ... destroying union halls ... loading strikers on the trains, shipping them out into the wilderness and dumping them. Of course, the strikers didn't always go along peaceably ... they liked living in town, you know, with their families. ...

The war was over the 8 hour work day, the Colorado Legislature had passed an 8 hour work law but unfortunately the governor, the mine owners, and the militia didn't agree ... and that's the way I wrote it, and the *New York American* printed it, on page 18 ... I got a wire from the editor saying he wasn't interested in politics, said he wanted headlines ... headlines.

(Narrator exits.)

HAYWOOD: *(Speaking primarily to the judge, who is standing next to the witness box.)* ... Well, we had been sitting playing cards for a couple of hours and suddenly as I was about to leave I noticed all of us had something in common, all five of us only had one eye. Ha, ha, ha. ...
VANDERVEER: I guess that's all for now. Your witness.
LANDIS: There will be a five minute recess. Mr. Nebeker, I'd like to speak to you please.

(Haywood leaves the stand, he, Vanderveer, and Doran come together in the center of the court room; all others exit.)

VANDERVEER: Bill, I thought you lost that eye when you were a kid, playing with a jack knife.
HAYWOOD: Who told you that?
VANDERVEER: Well, I think you did.
HAYWOOD: No, you musta heard that from one of the boys ... maybe Doran told you that.
VANDERVEER: No, you told me Bill.
DORAN: Yah! Why don't you tell him the truth? Everybody knows you lost it in a fight in some whore house in Wichita.

(Doran exits.)

HAYWOOD: Don't start ugly rumors. I only lost one eye. You know how bad conditions are in the mines, it musta, been in a mining accident. Doran, wait a minute.

(Haywood exits.)

VANDERVEER: Bill, you're on the stand, under oath, you can't be telling stories ...

(Vanderveer exits.)

SCENE TWO

(Outside the Silver Nugget Saloon, Cripple Creek, Colorado.)

TUSSY: I'm geting tired of this strike, I'll tell you that. We ain't gettin' no where but poor.
HOOTEN: Well, we ain't going back to work 'til the law is obeyed and the law says 8 hours.
TUSSY: Ain't nobody talking about going back to work. We're talking about doing something for ourselves.
HOOTEN: Tussy, you know what Bill said about talk like that!
TUSSY: ... he's been in Denver for too damn long. He start forgettin' what it's like out here.

(Haywood enters.)

HAYWOOD: Howdy, Boys.
TUSSY: Bill, Bill, how you doin'? Come on over here, what happened at the meeting, we been waitin'. . . .
HAYWOOD: Negotiating committee met with all the mine owners' people today . . . had an agreement hammered out to go back to work . . . 8 hours . . . $3.50 . . . but McNeill wouldn't go along . . . pressured all the others into backing him up, so we're gonna' have to stay out a little longer.
TUSSY: McNeill, you know he's shippin' so many scabs in here. . . . every day . . . he had to have extra cattle cars put on. But don't you worry about nothin', Bill, we know how to handle him and his scabs. . . .
HAYWOOD: You know there are times, we got to put up with scabs; there are times we get too hungry, we even got to do a little scabbing ourselves.
TUSSY: Yeah! But there ain't never no time when we have to put up with no spies. Me and Hoot caught us a spy today, cracked his skull and ran him out of town . . . ha . . . ha . . . ha.
HAYWOOD: Who was he? What was his name?
TUSSY: Never did catch his name . . . ha . . . ha . . . ha.
HAYWOOD: Well, I guess we can get away with a little rough stuff with a two-bit spy. . . .
TUSSY: Yeah, that two-bit McNeill is gonna' see a little of it too, ha . . . ha . . . ha.

(Haywood is suddenly very serious, grabbing Tussy.)

HAYWOOD: What does that mean, Tussy?

(Tussy realizes he has slipped.)

TUSSY: Well... uh... I just heard some of the boys are planning on bushwacking him.
HAYWOOD: Some of the boys, huh? Well, you find some of the boys and you TELL them why we lose strikes, because some idiot started shooting when he should have been thinking... if the governor sends the troops in here I'm commin' looking for YOU, TUSSY!
HOOTEN: Bill, we can't be watching all our people all the time.
HAYWOOD: Hoot, you know better than anyone, you were in the bull-pens, if the troops come in here, we will lose this strike... try and get that through his head.

(Haywood exits.)

HOOTEN: You know he's right, Tussy.
TUSSY: Yeah! Maybe... but if he ain't, maybe it's time we let the cat loose.

(Showing three sticks of dynamite.)

HOOTEN: You remember what he said about the troops....
TUSSY: I remember, I ain't stupid, but I'm gettin' damn tired of being kicked around. If things don't get better soon....

(Tussy exits. Hooten shakes his head, looks in the direction that Haywood exited and then in the direction that Tussy exited.)

HOOTEN: Tussy... Tussy....

(Hooten exits, trying to catch up with Tussy.)

SCENE THREE

NARRATOR: Well, it wasn't long before my editor got all the headlines he wanted... it was called the Colorado Civil War, half the mines in the state were blown up... even an ex-governor was killed... The mine owners tried to pin the whole thing on Bill... they hired the Pinkertons to kidnap him... shipped him off to Boise, Idaho for trial. That was in 1907, this time I was working for the *New York Call*, papers from all over the world were there, couldn't get near the telegraph office... miners came from all over the west... more Pinkertons than you could shake a stick at... of course... the militia was there, you know, keeping order... now Haywood had been in and out of jails all over the west... but this time he was in real trouble and he knew it... so the Western Federation sent to Chicago for Clarence Darrow... best defense lawyer in the country... odds makers made it 4 to 1, State of Idaho.

(Narrator exits. Darrow enters.)

DARROW: I don't know, Bill, things are gettin' tough....
HAYWOOD: Cheer up, Clarence, we're the one's who are gonna' hang.
DARROW: I don't know, Bill, the pressure must be gettin' to me. They got two goons following me around, they open my mail, tap my phone....
HAYWOOD: Clarence, look, I'll get some of the boys to pay a little visit....
DARROW: No, don't bother.
HAYWOOD: No trouble at all....
DARROW: NO, please... I'm putting you on the stand tomorrow, but I don't want any rough stuff, no politics, no nothing. Just sit and answer my questions, you can understand that....
HAYWOOD: Listen, Darrow....
DARROW: I don't want to hear it, Bill, this is a murder trial, get that through your head... you weren't arrested for loitering, this time....
HAYWOOD: Listen, Darrow, this is a political trial, that's why I wanted Debs here, that's why I wanted to get this out in the open to the workers....
DARROW: Debs??? Look at this, "Arouse ye slaves, the crisis has

come . . . if they attempt to murder Haywood . . . a million revolutionists will meet them with guns. . . ." Do you think we can win in Boise, Idaho with that, is that what you want to pin your defense on?

HAYWOOD: You were hired to be my lawyer, not my mentor! There are important political issues here, that you are not dealing with. They are trying to destroy the Western Federation. There is a conspiracy between the mine owners and the state officials to get rid of us . . . that's what you pin the defense on.

DARROW: Is that what you want? 'Cause if you do you'll drag the whole Federation down with you. . . .

HAYWOOD: I want Debs. . . .

DARROW: You got him. There's a train leaving for Chicago at 7 o'clock . . . I checked the time table. Make up your mind. . . .

(Haywood submits.)

DARROW: . . . I got some papers I want you to look over. . . .

(Lights focus on Darrow; he speaks to audience.)

DARROW: There's no doubt that Haywood is completely innocent in the Steunenberg killing, but what I've come to realize is that I don't like Bill Haywood. He believes in force and has used force. I'm certain that he is guilty of many acts of violence against property rather than persons, crimes well-provoked, but nonetheless crimes which will lead the labor movement down the wrong path.

(Pause.)

He's so damn sure of himself. Once he said, "I'd like to blast every mine owner out of the State of Colorado" and it's certain he would if he could. I can't go along with that, I'm a pacifist, I won't tolerate violence.

HAYWOOD: *(Angry and speaking to audience.)* Darrow's a brilliant lawyer and we stand side by side in that court room, but we really don't see eye to eye. Someone I do see eye to eye with is Gene Debs, one of the greatest socialists in this country. I wanted Debs here; I wanted rallies; I wanted mass meetings; I wanted a vigil ringing the court house; Debs could do all that and more, you can talk to that man, he listens and he understands the workers' struggle. That's why I wanted him here, I have searched my mind for Darrow's objections to Debs. Maybe he just wants all the limelight for himself.

(Darrow is speaking to the jury, but he speaks to the audience.)

DARROW: I want to speak to you plainly. Mr. Haywood is not my greatest concern. Wherever men have looked upward and onward, forgotten their selfishness, struggled for humanity, worked for the poor and the weak, they have been sacrificed. They have been sacrificed in the prisons, on the scaffold, in the flame... If you kill him your act will be applauded by many; if you decree his death, amongst the spiders of Wall Street will go up paeans of praise. In almost every corner of the world, where men wish to get rid of agitators and disturbers, you will receive blessings and praise that you have killed him... But if you free him, out on our broad prairies, where men toil with their hands, out on the broad oceans, where men are sailing the ships, throughout our mills and factories, down deep under the earth, thousands of men, of women, of children, weary with care and toil, will silently thank you, as I do now....

(Darrow exits.)

SCENE FOUR

(Narrator enters.)

NARRATOR: Bill was acquitted, but that was Boise, Idaho in 1907, not here in Chicago in 1918 ... Now Darrow believed the problem with this case was that Haywood was running the defense, why Darrow even offered to help, said he helped write the Espionage Act in Washington, he should have known the loop-holes, but Bill turned him down, can you beat that?

(Narrator exits, during the narrator's speech the court room was filling up, Landis raps his gavel.)

LANDIS: Let's get going, Mr. Nebeker.
NEBEKER: Your Honor, before proceeding with the cross examination of this witness I would like to read into the record some of the songs the IWW uses to advocate violence. This organization sinks to the lowest levels by taking Christian hymns and American patriotic songs and by changing the words for their own sinister ends. Possibly the worst of all is their use of songs to advocate sabotage, as in this one: "I had a job once thrashing wheat, worked sixteen hours with hands and feet."

(The ensemble enters and picks up the tune of the song Nebeker is reading. They sing the song to the audience while Nebeker continues to read in pantomime.)

ENSEMBLE:

(To the tune of "Ta ra ra boom de ay".)

I had a job once threshing wheat, worked sixteen hours with hands and feet.
And when the moon was shining bright, they kept me working all the night.
One moonlight night, I hate to tell, I accidentally slipped and fell.
My pitchfork went right in between some cog wheels of that thresh machine.
Ta ra ra boom de ay

It made a noise that way.
And wheels and bolts and hay,
Went flying every way.
That stingy rube said, "Well
A thousand gone to hell"
But I did sleep that night
I needed it all right.
But still that rube was pretty wise, these things did open up his eyes.
He said, "There must be something wrong, I think I work my men too long."
He cut the hours and raised the pay, gave ham and eggs for every day.
Now gets his men from union hall, and has no accidents at all.
Ta ra ra boom de ay
That rube is feeling gay.
He learned his lesson quick,
Just through a simple trick.
For fixing rotten jobs
And fixing greedy slobs,
This is the only way
Ta ra ra boom de ay.

(The ensemble crosses on the song and resumes their places in the jury box.)

NEBEKER: "This is the only way, ta ra ra boom de ay." I think that I will have the rest of the songs read into the record later, and get on with the cross-examination of Mr. Haywood.

(Nebeker motions to Haywood to take the stand; he does.)

NEBEKER: Now, Mr. Haywood, it seems that labor disturbances and violence have followed you throughout your infamous career... and not just with the IWW, but even earlier with the Western Federation of Miners. You were involved with the Cripple Creek Strike, weren't you Mr. Haywood?

HAYWOOD: Yes, I was there.

NEBEKER: When the miners decided to take over the mines?

HAYWOOD: They didn't try to take over the mines. They just walked out. Those men were working twelve hours a day, in total violation of the eight hour law.

NEBEKER: Come now, Mr. Haywood, weren't the authorities aware of this condition?

HAYWOOD: Oh, yes, indeed.

NEBEKER: Was the law inoperative, or... Why else wouldn't they prosecute the officials?
HAYWOOD: You're an attorney for the Justice Department, did you ever hear of a mine owner being prosecuted for violation of a law that protects a miner?
NEBEKER: Well, anyway, there was trouble between the mine owners of Colorado and the Western Federation of Miners?
HAYWOOD: Yes, there was.
NEBEKER: Trouble began, the trouble began about the time you landed in Colorado in 1901, didn't it?
HAYWOOD: No, the trouble began long before that, in 1880, the first strike was in Leadville... and there was a strike in Cripple Creek in 1894.
NEBEKER: Well....
HAYWOOD: There was also the Leadville strike of 1896.
NEBEKER: Yes, but....
HAYWOOD: There was also the mill strike of 1899.
NEBEKER: (*Unable to get in a word.*)
HAYWOOD: ...All those strikes had taken place before I came to Colorado.
NEBEKER: But things did start to really pick up as soon as you did get there, didn't they? Who was the Governor of Idaho at the time of the Coeur D'Alene trouble?
HAYWOOD: Steunenberg... Governor Steunenberg.
NEBEKER: Did anything happen to Governor Steunenberg?
HAYWOOD: He was blown up.
NEBEKER: Blown up? Could you be a little more specific?
HAYWOOD: Well, from what I was told, he was coming out of his house and when he opened the gate of his picket fence there was an explosion and he was killed.
NEBEKER: You were indicted for that murder? Weren't you?
VANDERVEER: I object. Haywood was acquitted of all connection with that crime.
LANDIS: Sustained.
VANDERVEER: Jesus Christ....
LANDIS: Continue, Mr. Nebeker.
NEBEKER: So, Governor Steunenberg was, as you say, BLOWN UP after his stand against the Western Federation... Is that right?
HAYWOOD: That happened years after the Coeur D'Alene fight.
NEBEKER: How long after, Mr. Haywood?
HAYWOOD: Oh, I don't know... six years... about six years.
NEBEKER: But isn't that one of the mottos of your organization... "We Never Forget?"

HAYWOOD: Are you referring to the IWW?
NEBEKER: The IWW.
HAYWOOD: It was not even in existence at that time.
NEBEKER: But isn't that one of the slogans of the IWW: "We Never Forget?"
HAYWOOD: That has ... that is not a slogan ... it has been the sort of ... words that have been used. ...
NEBEKER: Isn't it in your papers, and in your pamphlets, and on the stickers, and in thousands of places in the literature and writings of your organization?
HAYWOOD: Let me tell you where it was first used. ...
NEBEKER: Just answer the question, first.
HAYWOOD: Yes ... Now let me tell you where it was first used.
NEBEKER: Well, when did you first use it?
HAYWOOD: I first used it on a program for the funeral of Joe Hill, in 1915.
DORAN: Amen!
NEBEKER: The first time?
HAYWOOD: Yes, the first time.
NEBEKER: Are you sure? Didn't you also use that phrase while you were a member of the Western Federation of Miners?
HAYWOOD: I don't believe so. No.
NEBEKER: No? ... Well, I say you did.

(Nebeker picks up a newspaper from exhibit box.)

NEBEKER: WE NEVER FORGET, this was published in nineteen-hundred and twelve.

(Nebeker hands paper to jury.)

NEBEKER: And isn't it also true that the violence used and fostered by the Western Federation of Miners developed into the very basis of the IWW?
VANDERVEER: I object. That has nothing to do with. ...
LANDIS: Overruled.
HAYWOOD: ... The Western Federation never did anything more violent than protect themselves, their families, and their jobs. Those miners were being. ...
NEBEKER: Thank you, Mr. Haywood.
HAYWOOD: Judge ... where the hell is he ... I thought you wanted to hear this, Judge?

LANDIS: (*Seated behind Doran at defense table.*) Yes, I do, go ahead, William.

HAYWOOD: You see, the miners were on strike in one section of Colorado and the mill workers were on strike in another. The mill men were scabbing in the mines and the miners were scabbing in the mills ... They were destroying each others' unions. That was the basis for the one big union.

NEBEKER: That's all very interesting, Mr. Haywood. However, I'm talking about the thousands of documented cases of violence and sabotage committed by the IWW and the WFM and all the other radicals you are associated with.

VANDERVEER: I object. There is no evidence....

LANDIS: Overruled.

NEBEKER: I'm talking about the blowing up of Governor Steunenberg, the shooting of Mr. Frick, the blowing up of numerous mines and mills ... the blowing up of the *Los Angeles Times* ... Isn't this the kind of violence you advocate? Don't you want to destroy the existing order of things and doesn't that require violence? Don't you believe in extremes, violent extremes, Mr. Haywood?

VANDERVEER: I object.

HAYWOOD: I'll answer that, Van. The IWW advocates violence of the most violent sort ... violence that consists of keeping our mouths shut and our hands in our pockets. In doing this and staying on strike we are committing the most violent of acts ... cutting off our labor ... it is the most violent act we can commit against the capitalist, for it hurts him in his bank account, the only heart he has.

NEBEKER: Thank you, Mr. Haywood.

HAYWOOD: But don't get me wrong, we are against the blood in the streets kind of violence ... those actions come out of a feeling of impotence ... and we wouldn't be here today if we were impotent, would we Mr. Prosecutor?

(*Haywood has taken control and Landis, seeing this, bangs his gavel several times.*)

LANDIS: Court's adjourned 'til Monday morning at 9 A.M.

(*All exit.*)

SCENE FIVE

(Narratar enters.)

NARRATOR: Nebeker was no fool... to hear him talk... thousands of cases of violence... destroying the existing order... German gold in IWW pockets... it seems to me this war has got people so worked up they don't know what to think. Even Darrow, why he said, "While pacifism as a principle was fine during times of peace, it was not worth a hoot in hell during war time." But not Bill, he's always been consistent. He's always believed workers should not shoulder arms against each other. Bill didn't care if they were German or American, to him a worker was a worker... that was a cornerstone of the IWW founding convention at Brandt Hall, right here in Chicago in 1905.

(Haywood has moved to the table; he has a piece of lumber which he uses as a gavel.)

HAYWOOD: Fellow workers... This is the Continental Congress of the working class. It has been said that the purpose of this convention was to form an organization to rival Sam Gomper's A F of L. That is a mistake. We are here for the purpose of organizing a LABOR organization. There are A F of L locals that refuse to admit a colored man, that refuse to admit foreigners, that totally refuse to organize women or children, they have made America the land of the lost strike... their high initiation fees... their caste system... and their partnership with capital. What we want to establish at this time is an organization that will open wide its doors to every man or woman that earns his livelihood by brain or muscle. I don't give a snap of my fingers whether skilled workers join this union or not. We don't need them... there are 35 million workers in this country that aren't organized yet... and it does not make a damn bit of difference whether he is black or white, an American or a foreigner. For I am still of the opinion that an American is just as good as a foreigner, so long as he behaves himself... Thank you. This is your convention, so make the most of it. Come on boys!

(Ensemble enters and sings to the tune of "The Rambling Wreck from Georgia Tech.")

ENSEMBLE:
>We're anarchists and socialists and dynamiters too,
>We're the slaves of Wobbly delegates that tell us what to do;
>There's nothing we should kick about, we all got gall sublime,
>But we're bone and sinew of the land about election time.
>
>We're wild-eyed hayseeds, lazy shirks, agitators, knaves,
>We're looters of the vaults of wealth and our speaker
>   always raves;
>We're a danger to our country and republic all the time,
>But we're honest, sturdy farmers about election time.
>
>Yes, we're valiant hosts of labor about election time.
>We're thinking toilers of the land about election time.
>
>*(Ensemble exits. Stage is empty.)*

SCENE SIX

(Hoover enters; he is standing around waiting. We hear Landis's first line off stage as he enters.)

LANDIS: Morning Joe, Cubs doing fine, looks like they'll be in the series this year.

(Landis enters.)

HOOVER: Judge Landis? How do you do? My name's Hoover, special assistant to Attorney General Palmer.

(Landis walks.)

HOOVER: Sure is hot in Chicago this time of year. Cubs look like a winner this year.

(Landis stops and looks at Hoover.)

HOOVER: I hear you're a big fan.
LANDIS: Yah, it looks like they'll be in the series this year if their pitching holds out.
HOOVER: When do you think it will be over?
LANDIS: The season? That always runs into September....
HOOVER: No, the trial.
LANDIS: That's hard to say. It looks like they will be at each others' throats for a couple of months yet.
HOOVER: But, it's already July, that's almost four months gone by. People in Washington are getting a little concerned that this might drag on for too long. The country is getting worked up over these traitors. Real scum, you know.
LANDIS: Hoover, you got a lot to learn ... If Bill Haywood heard you, he'd kick your ass all the way back to Washington.
HOOVER: Attorney General Palmer sent me out here to....
LANDIS: Now, just wait a minute, Palmer's never presided over an IWW trial and I doubt if you've ever presided over anything. You see, this is my ball park, I'm the ump here, I make the calls.
HOOVER: Look, Judge Landis, we have already replaced one prosecutor, it's not out of the question to....

LANDIS: Now don't say something stupid, Hoover....

(Hoover starts to exit.)

LANDIS: HOOVER! Never underestimate people with a mission. Now I know what they're capable of and what their weaknesses are and I'm gonna' give them plenty of rope. When you're dealing with people with a cause you got to have respect.
HOOVER: Respect? What kind of respect....
LANDIS: No, not respect... affection... you know. I've really come to like some of these guys. You know when a visiting team comes into a ball park and they're hot, their pitcher has really got smoke on his fast ball and they're ready to clear the bench at any moment, you can really appreciate a team like that.

(Hoover just shakes his head.)

HOOVER: This is all very interesting, but... are you aware that the Bolsheviks have overthrown the Tsar and there are revolutionists all over our country with similar intentions? This is not quite a baseball game, Judge Landis.
LANDIS: Hoover, you're hopeless. Just go home to Washington and tell Palmer everything is under control.
HOOVER: I'm not an errand boy; I was sent here with very clear instructions.
LANDIS: Good day, Mr. Hoover.

(Hoover exits. Narrator has been watching the end of the scene from the shadows.)

NARRATOR: The truth, the whole truth and nothing but the truth... so help me God... You know, the truth is a funny thing... Sometimes you have to dig for it and sometimes it hits you right in the face. I once worked for a socialist editor... he told me... never see a striker hit a scab... always see the scab hit the striker... you see, there were seven or eight papers printing it the other way... he thought he'd keep the balance... at least he was honest with me.

(Court is called to order as court room fills up.)

LANDIS: Mr. Vanderveer, call your next witness.
VANDERVEER: I call Mr. J. T. Doran for the defense.

(Doran is sworn in and takes the stand.)

VANDERVEER: When did you come into the Industrial Workers of the World?
DORAN: As soon as I discovered they were in existence.
VANDERVEER: What was the reason for your going into the Industrial Workers of the World at that time?
NEBEKER: I object, Your Honor, we have been through all this before, the defendant's motivation is of no significance in this case.
VANDERVEER: Your Honor, the defendant is going to tell the jury first-hand what the IWW advocates.
LANDIS: Sit down, Mr. Nebeker, let's hear what he's got to say.

(Landis gestures to continue.)

VANDERVEER: Tell us, Red, why did you join the IWW?
DORAN: Well, I had been around the country a good deal at my trade, and I found that conditions on the jobs were so poor that something had to be done.
VANDERVEER: What is your trade, Red?
DORAN: I earn my way as a mechanic, work on big engines, mining camps, lumber mills . . . but actually I'm a WPE.
VANDERVEER: WPE?
DORAN: Worker's Professor of Economics.
VANDERVEER: Now, we understand that you traveled around from camp to camp organizing, and made this presentation to educate the workers. When you went to make your talk, what subject did you talk on?
DORAN: Well, I used what I am pleased to call a chalk talk, using crude illustrations, a blackboard and a piece of chalk.

(Holding up a piece of chalk.)

VANDERVEER: The talk that you gave, was that substantially the same at the various places where you. . . .
DORAN: Always the same, that is, I did not recite it poll-parrot fashion, but the substance did not vary.
VANDERVEER: You're on, Mr. Doran.

(Vanderveer hands blackboard to Doran. Doran moves to stage center, smiles at the audience, raises and lowers his eyebrows several times, tries to see the faces of the people in the audience, smiles, takes a deep breath.)

DORAN: Compadres, Copanes, Kung Yow Moon, fellow-workers, you have heard a great deal about the IWW, and you know what people say about us. The sheets usually credit us with being a lot of murderers, a lot of irresponsible dynamiters and agitators. . . .

The IWW does not ask you as working men to do a single solitary thing that you do not already do. We ask you to do in the interest of humanity, in the interest of yourself and your wife and your babies, just what you now do in the interest of the economic waste, the profit-holders. Don't let me get away from you, you see, we IWW's suggest something. We suggest doing away with capitalism. Why? Because we find it objectionable. We suggest tearing it down, but we are not destructionists. We propose to tear it down, but we propose to put something in its place and what is that thing we propose to put up in its place? Socialism. Now, don't get scared! 'Cause before you can understand socialism, you got to understand capitalism, the system under which you now work. And before you can understand capitalism, you gotta' understand surplus value. That's right, surplus value, surplus, I say. So let's deal with surplus value. This here is a factory, a farm, a mine, a timber mill, any means of production.

(He draws a box on the board.)

Each and every one of you walks in in the morning and out at night.

(He draws lines going into the box and lines going out.)

And what do you get for your hard labor, for your sweat, for your dreary days and tired nights?

(He turns the lines coming out of the box into small dollar signs.)

Not much, wages they say, slave wages I say, a mere token, hardly enough to live on. Now that factory or mine makes big money.

(He draws a huge dollar sign at the bottom of the board beneath the box.)

On any day's shift a worker produces say two hundred dollars worth of goods. Thirty dollars go to overhead and materials...

(He draws a roof on the box and smoke coming out of the top.)

...Two dollars go to you... that leaves 168 dollars and what happens to those 168 dollars? That is the unpaid wages, the profits, the SURPLUS VALUE. Who gets that surplus value? Not you or me. What happened to it, we must have lost it.

(He turns board, looking for the 168 dollars.)

Under socialism, workers wouldn't lose that surplus value, it would be theirs, yours, because you would own the mine. Now someone might say the capitalists own the mines and have a right to keep them. But let me tell you a story about gold mines. The absentee owner did not find the gold, he did not mine the gold, he did not mill the gold, but by some strange alchemy, he owns the gold—all the gold belongs to him. Now think about that.

NEBEKER: This is a conspiracy to take from the owner what is constitutionally his and in the ownership of which the law supports him.

(During this interchange Doran erases drawing and draws a cartoon of Nebeker's face and writes "FOOL" under it.)

LANDIS: Please, Mr. Nebeker.

(Waving Nebeker to his seat.)

NEBEKER: The wage system is established by law and all opposition to it is opposition to law.

LANDIS: Mr. Doran has an interesting theory, Mr. Nebeker, you must admit, although as irrelevant as the Holy Bible. Continue Mr. Doran.

DORAN: Now let's look at this from another angle.

(Flipping the chalk board over, there is a pyramid drawn on the board.)

DORAN: Now, this great mass of men and women on the bottom here, represented by this line, are the workers, their activities in any business are governed by another element known as the straw-boss element, they're just like you and me, but they have been bought off, they have been bribed, an extra half dollar. . . .

(He pulls a half dollar from the ear of a jury member.)

. . .and he looks out for the interests of the owners rather than himself. . . .

(Landis walks over to see better.)

DORAN: . . . and then supervising the activities of the straw-boss element is the foreman element, the push. Now it takes a little more to buy him off, maybe an extra dollar.

(Doran pulls a dollar out of Landis's pocket.)

Supervising the foreman is the general foreman, the superintendent, the manager, the general manager, and then the economic waste, the profit-holders, the bond-holders, the people who do not do anything, and that is where the surplus value goes. Gabish, Verstehen, Savvy, do you understand? I usually end by passing the hat, but considering the circumstances, I guess we can dispense with that today.
LANDIS: Yes, you can, Mr. Doran.
VANDERVEER: Your witness.

(Nebeker pauses, Doran sits, uneasy.)

NEBEKER: How many times have you been arrested, Doran?
DORAN: I have been persecuted and arrested a number of times, never tried.
NEBEKER: Answer my question, how many times have you been arrested?
DORAN: In Los Angeles they arrested me four or five times a week for months and never let me see a judge, Judge.
NEBEKER: How many times have you been arrested?
DORAN: I don't know, lots of times on that kind of charge, I was never convicted of a felony in my life.
NEBEKER: Have you been arrested a dozen times?
DORAN: Yes, several dozen times, at least.
NEBEKER: Could you repeat that?
DORAN: Several dozen times.

NEBEKER: In every case you were in the right and they were in the wrong, I suppose?
DORAN: They never tried me.
NEBEKER: Answer my question.
DORAN: I don't know, they never took it to a showdown; I presume I was right.
NEBEKER: So, you have been persecuted by the Justice Department?
DORAN: Yeah.
NEBEKER: Are you telling this court there is a conspiracy in the United States Government to persecute Mr. J. T. Doran?
DORAN: I say there is a capitalist conspiracy in this country to persecute the workers.
NEBEKER: So what you are really saying is that justice as it is in this country is capitalist justice?
DORAN. Yes.
NEBEKER: There is no justice for the workers in the courts?
DORAN: No.
NEBEKER: That all the courts are what you would call capitalist courts?
DORAN: Yes.
NEBEKER: You don't believe there is any justice to be had in this court, do you?
DORAN: I don't think I can get any justice from a Copper-Trust-dumb-lawyer-son-of-a-bitch like you.
NEBEKER: *(To Landis.)* Does this counsel have to put up with this low life?

(Doran goes for Nebeker, jumping over railing.)

DORAN: You miserable bastard, you know this whole trial is a big frame-up.

(Haywood restrains Doran; Vanderveer shaking his head walks off; Landis, enjoying himself, waves Nebeker back. Haywood tries to hold Doran.)

DORAN: Why don't you just hang me right now, like you hung Frank Little. You son-of-a-bitch, this ain't no trial, this is a lynch mob. The working class and the employing class have nothing in common. Bill, let go of me, Goddamn it....

General Construction Workers
DON'T TRUST to LUCK
JOIN The UNION
Industrial Union No. 310 of the I.W.W.

If you believe in such a superstition as "The Black Cat Crossing Your Trail Will Cause You Bad Luck" and are willing to trust to LUCK for job conditions, length of working hours and living standard in camp, you need not finish reading this leaflet. But if you realize that these things are entirely what you MAKE them and the "Benevolence of the Boss" is only what you force it to be, you will carefully consider the program of Union-controlled camps as set forth in this leaflet.

ACT TWO

SCENE ONE

(We are in a boxcar traveling toward the wheat fields, we hear the sounds of a train coming to a stop, the sun is just rising, the scrim is closed.)

LEN: Where are we, anyway?
SHORTY: Should be close to the North Dakota line by now.

(Shorty looks out the box car door, we hear off-stage the voice of an IWW organizer.)

IWW ORGANIZER: I'll take this one, you go two down.
SHORTY: Listen. . . .

(Hears whistling.)

SHORTY: Wobblies.
LEN: Who?
SHORTY: Wobblies, shhhhh, maybe they won't find us . . . come on, let's get out of here.

(They start to gather their things. The IWW organizer enters.)

IWW ORGANIZER: Heading for the harvest, fellows? Guess you know you can't ride no harvest-bound freighters without you joining the IWW . . . I'm an IWW delegate. Now listen to me and listen close. Take this harvest. If we're organized, we don't have to work for no lousy three or four bucks a day, like some in Minnesota. In Dakota, we don't work for less than six bucks . . . All right, you guys going to join up, or get out and walk?
LEN: How much is it?
IWW ORGANIZER: One dollar. Red Card's good for a year. You can ride on it any where.
LEN: I'd like to join, but all I got is a few nickels.

IWW ORGANIZER: Likely you got nothin' in your stomach but gas, yet you suckers think you can beat the system without organizing.

(IWW looks at Shorty.)

SHORTY: I'm broke too.
IWW ORGANIZER: Well, you could be flat at that. I know how it is. But wise up ... I'm gonna' let you ride this time. But first pay you get, you look up a Wobbly delegate and join, how about it?
SHORTY: All right, you got my word, first pay I'll join.
LEN: Sure thing, first pay.
IWW ORGANIZER: *(He hands them a paper.)* Here, read this, maybe it'll take your minds off your stomachs. Good luck, fellas ...

(IWW Organizer exits.)

SHORTY: Well, we got away with it.

(Shorty looks out to see where the IWW Organizer went, glances at the paper, then sets it down.)

LEN: What do you think of all this?
SHORTY: Of all what?
LEN: What the Wob guy said and what's in this sheet.
SHORTY: Well, it ain't all crap.

(They start to roll up their blankets.)

LEN: You gonna' join, like you said?
SHORTY: Could be. How's about you?
LEN: Sure, first chance. We ought'a stick together, right?
SHORTY: Go to it, but watch yourself, the Wobblies ain't so strong as they make out. Don't let the cops catch you with a red card. even the guys you work with. Don't let on 'til you're real sure. I know. I been a union man. What they done to us when we went on strike was a shame.
LEN: Yeah, I bet.
SHORTY: They got the right idea about all being in one union—not one union scabbin' on another like where I was ... and they ain't so wrong about what we could do if we stuck together. We could tie up any job tighter'n a cow's ass in flytime ... tie up the whole works. But I tell you what. That ain't never gonna

happen. You know why? 'Cause workin' men just won't stick together, no sir, they never done it and they never will.

(Len nods.)

LEN: I wonder how come.
SHORTY: Ah, come on, let's scare up something to eat.

(They exit.)

SCENE TWO

(The following scene is a montage which combines old photos projected on the scrim with actors in front of and behind the scrim. The slides constantly change as they illustrate the dialogue. Several lighting formats are used: projected photos can cover the entire scrim or just the left or right half, a tight spot behind the scrim can illuminate actors either through the blank scrim or through images projected on the scrim.)

VOICES:

"Guiseppi, did you get right pay?"
"No! What about you?"
"Short."
"Short pay."
"Cut the belts."
"Leave, everyone leave, we walk out."
"Strike, strike!"

> *(Workers begin to chant, as the volume of the chants rise the volume of the factory noises decreases, we hear sounds of sabotage.)*

> *(MONTAGE of photos of picket lines, workers leaving factories, police, fire hoses.)*

> *(Stage right, Elizabeth Gurley Flynn begins to speak, two workers appear and simultaneously translate her speech into Italian and a Slavic tongue. Special light stage right allows us to see her through scrim with slide filling other half of scrim.)*

FLYNN: Fellow workers, the bosses refer to you as mill hands . . . farm hands, factory hands . . . a boss would feel insulted if you called him a hand, he's a head . . . the trouble is he owns your head and your hands . . . but there is something you can do about that . . . STRIKE! STRIKE!

> *(Lights and slides change, we see Wood through scrim, stage left.)*

WILLIAM WOOD: Go back to work . . . get back to work. Listen to me. Be quiet and listen to me. Thank you. I'm William Wood. I own the American Woolen Company, so I guess I should know what's going on in Lawrence. There has been a misunderstanding. You have to understand, there are no excessive profits coming to the textile manufacturers of Massachusetts. On the contrary, for many of these businesses there are no profits at all. Many are in dire trouble. You used to work 56 hours a week. Now, the law says that women and children can work only 54 hours a week. To pay for 54 hours work the wages of 56 would be the equivalent of an increase in wages that the mills cannot afford to pay.

(Lights and slide change back to Flynn at stage right.)

FLYNN: Let me read you something . . . net profits four million dollars . . . dividends three million . . . total surplus eleven million. Now does that sound like no profits at all? That 54 hour law was passed to benefit you. But the companies saw a way to make it benefit them, by speeding up the machines. But we're not going to stand for it, are we? Let's make this the biggest textile strike in history. I'm Elizabeth Gurley Flynn from the Industrial Workers of the World. Eight hours of work, eight hours of play, eight hours of sleep, and eight dollars a day!

(Full slide covers scrim. We hear picket line song through scrim.)

(Sung to the tune of "In the Good Old Summer Time.")

In the good old picket line, in the good old picket line
The workers are from every place, from nearly every clime.
The Greeks and the Poles are out so strong,
       and the Germans all the time.
But we want to see more Irish in the good old picket line.

In the good old picket line, in the good old picket line,
We'll put Mr. Wood in overalls and swear off drinking wine.
Then Gurley Flynn will be the boss,
       Oh, gee, won't that be fine.
The strikers will wear diamonds in the good old picket line.

(Lights go on small table, stage left, with woman seated at it, slides continue on scrim stage right illustrating her testimony.)

VOICE: The House Committee on Rules hearing into the strike at Lawrence, Massachusetts, will come to order.

(Gavel raps.)

CONGRESSMAN BERGER: What is your name, please?
SHAPLEY: Dr. Elizabeth Shapley.
CONGRESSMAN BERGER: How do you come to have pertinent information for this committee?
SHAPLEY: I am a social worker and have recently completed an investigation into Lawrence for the United States Labor Commissioner.
CONGRESSMAN BERGER: What have you found to be the working and living conditions in and around Lawrence?
SHAPLEY: There are 22,000 textile employees, who average $8.76 for a full week's work. Rents range from $1.00 to $6.00 a week for small tenement apartments which are fire traps.
CONGRESSMAN BERGER: Who owns the buildings?
SHAPLEY: Most of the tenements are owned by the mills. Mill families find it necessary to take in boarders in order to eat.
CONGRESSMAN BERGER: Well, with this additional income, do these people have an adequate diet?
SHAPLEY: If you call bread, molasses, and beans an adequate diet. Meat is certainly a luxury.
CONGRESSMAN BERGER: Who makes up the work force at these mills?
SHAPLEY: Half of all the workers in the Lawrence Mills are young girls. A considerable number of the boys and girls die within the first two or three years after beginning work. Because of malnutrition, work strain, and occupational diseases. Thirty-five out of every hundred mill workers die before they are twenty-five years of age.
CONGRESSMAN BERGER: How many nationalities are there represented among the workers at Lawrence?
SHAPLEY: Approximately sixteen.
CONGRESSMAN BERGER: Do they speak English?
SHAPLEY: Oh, no. They're all foreigners.

(Lights change back to stage right, where Haywood is standing.)

HAYWOOD: There are no foreigners here, to the working class there are no foreigners but the bosses. Do not let them divide you by sex, color, creed, or nationality. Billy Wood can lick one Pole, in fact, he can lick all the Poles, but Billy Wood cannot lick the ... *(He ticks off the nationalities on his fingers.)* ... Poles, Italians, Irish, Jews, Lithuanians ... when they stand together ... And let's not forget the A F of L ... this is the way the A F of L organizes. ... *(He holds up the other hand and ticks off the trades on his fingers.)* ... by separating weavers ... loom fixers ... spinners ... carders. This is the way the IWW organizes ... together ... *(He clenches both fists.).*

(Lights change back to small table, stage left, where we see Berger and Golden.)

CONGRESSMAN BERGER: Mr. Golden, you are the president of the United Textile Workers of the A F of L.

GOLDEN: Yes, sir.

CONGRESSMAN BERGER: Mr. Golden, if these wage-earners had been American citizens, all of them speaking the English language, would this trouble have occurred?

GOLDEN: I think, Mr. Chairman, the best answer to that is this: of the thousands of organized workers in the United Textile Workers in Massachusetts, we did not have a single one go out on strike.

CONGRESSMAN BERGER: Could you then tell us why your men are working and these people in Lawrence are on strike?

GOLDEN: The United Textile workers would have negotiated, talked, sat down and worked out our differences. By now, you do not have a strike in Lawrence, you have a revolution there.

(Lights go out, we see a slide that fills the scrim, and we hear song from behind scrim. During song slides continue.)

> A little talk with Golden
> Makes it right, all right
> He'll settle any strike
> If there's coin enough in sight
> Just take him up to dine
> And everything is fine
> A little talk with Golden
> Makes it right, all right.

The preachers, cops, and money kings were
                                   working hand in hand
The boys in blue, with stars and stripes,
                                   were sent by Uncle Sam
Still things were looking blue 'cause every striker knew

> That weaving cloth with bayonets is hard to do.
> A little talk with Golden
> *(repeat chorus above.)*

(Lights come up on stage right, where we see Haywood standing.)

HAYWOOD: Golden now says you shouldn't have gone out, but did he admit you to his union? No, the United Textile Workers has never organized the foreign-born and they oppose your strike now. And look at your children!

(Lights change back to small table, stage left.)

CONGRESSMAN BERGER: Right this way, please....

(Girl comes in.)

CONGRESSMAN BERGER: Thank you for coming.
CAMELLA TEOLI: You're welcome....
CONGRESSMAN BERGER: What is your name?
CAMELLA TEOLI: Camella Teoli....
CONGRESSMAN BERGER: And how old are you?
CAMELLA TEOLI: Eight years....
CONGRESSMAN BERGER: Where do you go to school?
CAMELLA TEOLI: I don't go to school ... I'm through with school ... I work.
CONGRESSMAN BERGER: You work ... Where do you work?
CAMELLA TEOLI: In the woolen mill.
CONGRESSMAN BERGER: For the American Woolen Company?
CAMELLA TEOLI: Yes.
CONGRESSMAN BERGER: What sort of work do you do?
CAMELLA TEOLI: My work is to take off empty bobbins and put full bobbins on.

CONGRESSMAN BERGER: Could you show the committee how you do that?
CAMELLA TEOLI: Like this....

(She demonstrates.)

CONGRESSMAN BERGER: And what are your hours? How long do you work?
CAMELLA TEOLI: We work all day ... ten hours ... every day.

CONGRESSMAN BERGER: How much do you get a week?
CAMELLA TEOLI: About $6.00... If they don't take anything out.
CONGRESSMAN BERGER: What do they take out?
CAMELLA TEOLI: Well, if you make mistakes or something... or if you're late or sick... or for drinking water...they take out five cents a week for drinking water.
CONGRESSMAN BERGER: They do not furnish you with drinking water?
CAMELLA TEOLI: No. They say it is spring water, but it is not... it's canal water.
CONGRESSMAN BERGER: Are you working now?
CAMELLA TEOLI: No. I was hurt.
CONGRESSMAN BERGER: In the mill?
CAMELLA TEOLI: Yes....
CONGRESSMAN BERGER: Can you tell the committee about that... how it happened?
CAMELLA TEOLI: I got hurt in my head....
CONGRESSMAN BERGER: What part of your head?
CAMELLA TEOLI: My head.
CONGRESSMAN BERGER: Well, how were you hurt?
CAMELLA TEOLI: The machine pulled the scalp off.
CONGRESSMAN BERGER: The machine pulled your scalp off?
CAMELLA TEOLI: Yes, sir....
CONGRESSMAN BERGER: Were you in the hospital after that?
CAMELLA TEOLI: I was in the hospital seven months....
CONGRESSMAN BERGER: Are you one of the strikers?
CAMELLA TEOLI: Yes, sir. I'm one of the strikers.

(Lights change back to stage right.)

HAYWOOD: I tell you that their little lives are woven into the woolen goods they weave... in those threads are twisted the tears and heartache of these little children. We have friends in other cities, that have offered to take care of our children until the strike is over. This is a good idea. The children will be better fed and clothed away from Lawrence. You talk among yourselves, speak with the delegates, we will vote on it tonight.

(Lights change back to small table, stage left.)

CONGRESSMAN BERGER: We have heard a good deal about the beating of women and children who were trying to board the trains, did you see any of these outrages that have been spoken of here? Did you see any of these women that were clubbed?

CAMELLA TEOLI: I did.
CONGRESSMAN BERGER: Tell me what you know about that.
CAMELLA TEOLI: I saw one of the policemen grab a lady by the throat and hit her on the head.
CONGRESSMAN BERGER: What did he hit her with?
CAMELLA TEOLI: A club.
CONGRESSMAN BERGER: A policeman's billy?
CAMELLA TEOLI: Yes, sir, a good club.
CONGRESSMAN BERGER: Could you tell us what happened?
CAMELLA TEOLI: They stopped us from getting on the train, then they started beating. I saw them take little kids and pick them up by the leg and throw them in the police wagon. One lady put up a fight and a policeman grabbed her by the neck and choked her until she was dead, I think.
CONGRESSMAN BERGER: Thank you.

(All lights behind scrim go out, stage clears, lights come up, we see Narrator in the court room, empty.)

SCENE THREE

NARRATOR: Through all this the spirit of the strike held fast. On March 12, 1912, sixty-three days after the workers had walked off their jobs, the mighty American Woolen Company speaking for all Lawrence mills collapsed and capitulated.

(Scrim opens, the court room fills up.)

NARRATOR: Bill said it was the women who won the strike. It was a singing strike, song overcame all language barriers, a new kind of strike. That got me thinkin' about my own job security... during those sixty-three days I worked... thirty-seven... for three different newspapers... you hang around with these Wobblies sure does turn your head around.

(A young man in Army uniform is on the stand. He is being questioned by Vanderveer.)

VANDERVEER: Your name is Otto Stolp?
STOLP: My name is Otto Stolp, yes sir.
VANDERVEER: Where do you live?
STOLP: Why, I am in the Army now, sir.
VANDERVEER: Where are you stationed?
STOLP: Fort Benjamin Harrison.
VANDERVEER: How many boys are out there in the camp with you?
STOLP: There are between twelve and eighteen-thousand.
VANDERVEER: And what class do they come from?
STOLP: Mostly all railroad men, where I am.
VANDERVEER: Railroad men, you mean presidents' sons, superintendents' sons?
STOLP: Why, no, Sir. They are mostly all working men.
VANDERVEER: Mostly all working men?
STOLP: Yes, Sir.
VANDERVEER: Where do you call home?
STOLP: Well, I have been making my home around Seattle the last ten years.
VANDERVEER: How old are you?
STOLP: Twenty-nine, Sir.
VANDERVEER: What line of work do you follow?

STOLP: I play the woods, Sir.
VANDERVEER: Play the woods?
STOLP: I work in a lumber camp.
VANDERVEER: Any particular kind of work?
STOLP: Brakeman on logging roads, Sir.
VANDERVEER: When did you join the IWW?
STOLP: July 3, 1917, Sir.
VANDERVEER: Do you believe in the IWW?
STOLP: Yes, Sir.
VANDERVEER: Feel the same about it now as you did when you joined it?
STOLP: Yes, Sir.
VANDERVEER: Mean to keep up your membership in it?
STOLP: Yes, Sir.
VANDERVEER: Good, that is all. Your witness.
NEBEKER: When did you join the Army, Private Stolp?
STOLP: June 1, 1918.
NEBEKER: Up to the time that you enlisted in 1918, did you read what the IWW papers, *Industrial Worker* and *Solidarity*, had to say about this war?
STOLP: I didn't see nothing in them against the war.
NEBEKER: What?
STOLP: I didn't read nothing against the war.
NEBEKER: Did you read anything about war, in any of their publications?
STOLP: Very little, Sir.
NEBEKER: Have you ever read any of the literature of the IWW?
STOLP: I have read some of it, yes, Sir.
NEBEKER: Have you read their books on sabotage?
STOLP: No, Sir.
NEBEKER: You would not practice sabotage in the Army, would you?
STOLP: I don't know what it is, Sir.

(Nebeker is taken aback by this, hesitates for a moment.)

NEBEKER: Now, would you believe in the IWW if their official papers called this war a capitalistic war and said that it was not the duty of working men to fight for this country in this war ... would you still believe in and be with it?
STOLP: How's that again, Sir?
NEBEKER: Didn't you follow the question, Private Stolp? I'll repeat it. If it were true that the IWW told you it was not the duty of

working men to fight for this country in this war, would you still belong to it?
STOLP: There is nothing but working men fighting in this war that I know of, Sir.
NEBEKER: Now did you follow my question? If that were true, would you still believe in it and adhere to it?
STOLP: Why, it isn't true, Sir.
LANDIS: Talk so we can hear you, Private Stolp.
STOLP: I don't know what he's getting at, Sir. I never read nothing like that in them papers.
NEBEKER: No, but I say if that were the case, if you could be shown that was the case, what would you do?
STOLP: Why, I would not stay with them then, no.
NEBEKER: No further questions.
VANDERVEER: Do you believe in war, Stolp?
STOLP: Why, I believe in getting the Kaiser, yes, Sir.
VANDERVEER: Well, that is so. But do you believe in war generally?
STOLP: No, Sir.
VANDERVEER: Do you know any IWWs who do not believe in getting the Kaiser?
STOLP: I do not, Sir.
VANDERVEER: What is the attitude of the IWW about war generally?
STOLP: All I have ever talked with, wanted to go and get this war settled with, get the Kaiser.
VANDERVEER: Have you ever given any thought to the subject of the causes of the war?
STOLP: No, Sir, I have not.
VANDERVEER: Do you know what remedy the IWW proposes as a preventative for war, what measures?
STOLP: No, I do not, Sir.
VANDERVEER: Thank you.
NEBEKER: Your heart and soul is in this war?
STOLP: Yes, Sir.
NEBEKER: And you are fighting loyally for your country, are you?
STOLP: Yes, Sir.
NEBEKER: And your heart and soul is in the IWW?
STOLP: Yes, Sir.
NEBEKET: Are you fighting loyally for that?
STOLP: Fighting for both, yes, Sir.
NEBEKER: You don't know much about the IWW, do you?
STOLP: Well, I have belonged to them and I do now.
NEBEKER: But, have you read much about them?

STOLP: I did not have the time, Sir, to read before we got the eight hours, I was working all the time.
NEBEKER: That is all.
VANDERVEER: Do you know what the preamble says, that the working class and employing class have nothing in common?
STOLP: Yes, Sir. Nothing in common.
VANDERVEER: You know that is the cornerstone of the IWW?
STOLP: Yes, Sir.
VANDERVEER: Well, now, what makes you believe it, what is there about it?
STOLP: I know they have nothing in common because of the way I have been pushed around through the country.
VANDERVEER: You have never had an employer worry about the condition of your health or your morals?
STOLP: No, Sir, never did.
VANDERVEER: Never know them to worry about how the women of you working people get along?
STOLP: They don't seem to care.
VANDERVEER: Whether your babies live or die?
STOLP: They don't care, no, Sir.
VANDERVEER: Or whether you become good citizens or bad citizens?
STOLP: Never.
VANDERVEER: Whether you are educated or not?
STOLP: They never care.
VANDERVEER: Are those the things that you refer to as the class war, the war for the betterment of those things?
STOLP: Yes, Sir, that is what we want to do.
VANDERVEER: Now, do you think it is loyal to this country to try to remedy those things?
STOLP: Yes, Sir, it is.
VANDERVEER: I guess that's all.
NEBEKER: Just a question... Is it your view that the employers as a class and as individuals have no common interest with you in this war?
STOLP: Why, they don't seem to, no.
NEBEKER: You do not know any who have enlisted?
STOLP: No, Sir.
NEBEKER: Have you been taught to believe that the sons of employers are not enlisting to fight the battles of their country?
STOLP: Taught?... in school.... no, Sir, it's just that I don't know of any, Sir.
NEBEKER: I think that's all.

VANDERVEER: You said a few moments ago that you thought the workers were fighting the war.
STOLP: That is who it is, Sir.
VANDERVEER: Any other IWWs?
STOLP: Oh! Yes, Sir, plenty of them, Sir.
VANDERVEER: Do you see any of these capitalists fighting it?
STOLP: I haven't seen none, no, Sir.
VANDERVEER: Well, how do you feel about having people like that say that you and your brothers are not patriotic?
STOLP: Well, Sir, what I feel is that . . . sometimes it just don't seem fair . . . why they should put a uniform on their backs and come right along with us, show their patriotism, get the Kaiser!
VANDERVEER. Thank you, Stolp. That'll be all.

(Stolp looks at Nebeker, who waves him off. Stolp leaves the stand and goes to the defense table to shake hands with Haywood and Doran, then exits. Landis calls Nebeker and Vanderveer to the bench.)

HAYWOOD: He's all right, he really told them, now after the war. . . .
DORAN: He ain't gonna' live that long. Get the Kaiser! Get the Kaiser! Crap . . . we should have taken a real stand against the war.
HAYWOOD: What are you talking about, they would have destroyed us.
DORAN: Just what the hell do you think is gonna' happen now! They're gonna' let us rot in here; it's better to fight and go out in a blaze of glory than this horse shit.
HAYWOOD: We couldn't stop the war; the class war is our fight, not the World War, our job is to organize and prepare for the general strike. . . .
DORAN: For what? The general strike, the general strike, just when is that supposed to happen, pie in the sky, bullshit. I say now, let's have the son-of-a-bitch now! We got thousands of members, why we could shut down the whole country.
HAYWOOD: We got to bide our time.
DORAN: Look, Bill, ten million have died already; we got to do something, maybe we could at least save that sap's life.
HAYWOOD: I don't know.
DORAN: We ain't nothin' anymore; you're still living on past glories, you know that. . . .
VANDERVEER: Doran, come on. . . .
DORAN: Look, we're goin' under.
VANDERVEER: Just lay off. . . .

DORAN: Lay off, you see what's. . . .
VANDERVEER: Lay off, just lay off. . . .

(Doran exits; Vanderveer exits. Haywood sits alone, rises slowly and exits. Narrator enters, picking up Doran's paper from the defense table.)

SCENE FOUR

NARRATOR: Armies clash at Verdun in globe's greatest battle... Bonds buy bullets, buy bonds... Oh! the daily casualty list... General Pershing reported the lowest for the week... 98... well, I guess that's low, if your name isn't on it. It seems to me, we just elected Wilson president to keep us out of this war, sure am glad we didn't get... the other one... what's his name... To date the American Protective League working hand in hand with the Department of Justice has ferreted out and brought to justice three million cases of disloyalty. I wonder how they missed me...and they are only ONE patriotic group, there's also the American Defense Society, the Home Defense League, the Liberty League, the Knights of Liberty, the Anti-Yellow Dog League, the terrible theateners, the sedition slammers, and the Boy Spies of America....

Hey, Ex-Governor Campbell's back in the news; now he's the guy who showed up at this trial with a suitcase full of evidence proving the IWW was getting funds from Germany, He's been standing around with his suitcase waiting to be called as a witness. But today he suddenly announced that the famous suitcase had been stolen by an IWW posing as a Pullman Porter. Now, if you believe that, the Boy Spies of America sure has an opening for you.

(Narrator exits; Landis followed by Hoover enter talking.)

LANDIS: *(Off stage.)* Morning, John, yeah, they'll be in the series this year. *(On stage to Hoover.)* Hoover, don't you ever give up?
HOOVER: People in Washington have been very impressed with how you have dealt with radicals in the past.
LANDIS: Well, if they're so impressed, what are you doing here? I told you last time that I would handle this.
HOOVER: Yes... but I thought we had an understanding.
LANDIS: What exactly, do you think I can do for you, Mr. Hoover?
HOOVER: I have conducted nationwide raids on this group, I have two other trials planned, I had the post office cut off their mail service, I personally spoke to the Attorney General himself....
LANDIS: You're a busy man, do you sell Liberty Bonds on the side, too?

51

HOOVER: Landis, this is serious, I have plans for ... the Attorney General has plans for an even greater crack-down as soon as you get this trial over with ... but, we are still waiting.
LANDIS: Well, while you are waiting, why don't you enlist, get the Kaiser, and when you come back. ...
HOOVER: Judge Landis, time is of the essence; we have got to get this over with.

(Landis, by now, is at the bench; he looks down on Hoover.)

LANDIS: Mr. Hoover, what exactly is your hurry?
HOOVER: It's very simple, the war may be over soon and people will quickly forget about the reds in this country.

(Landis comprehends.)

LANDIS: I appreciate what you've told me and we are all doing our parts. Good day, Mr. Hoover.
HOOVER: Good day, Judge Landis.

(Hoover exits. Doran enters.)

DORAN: Hi, ya, Judge, who's your friend? Looks like a fed to me, ah, but you never can tell. I just wanted to tell ya that the boys really appreciate the fair trial you're giving us, the way you're taking care of us, letting us speak our piece ... you been a regular Jake-cat.
LANDIS: What was that?
DORAN: Jake-cat ... a good guy ... you're all right, Judge.
LANDIS: Thank you, Red.

(Court fills up. Landis raps gavel.)

LANDIS: Mr. Nebeker, I believe you were in the process of calling witnesses for re-cross examination.
NEBEKER: Thank you, Your Honor, I call Mr. Doran for recross.

(Doran takes the stand.)

NEBEKER: Mr. Doran, were you at the IWW convention in 1916?

(Doran is silent.)

NEBEKER: Mr. Doran, did you vote on the war resolution at that convention?

(Doran smiles at Landis.)

NEBEKER: Tell me, Mr. Doran, what's your position on the war?

(Doran is silent.)

NEBEKER: Do you support the declaration of war against Imperial Germany?

(Doran is calm, smiling and silent.)

NEBEKER: Haven't got much to say today, huh? Are you gonna' answer any of my questions?

(Doran says nothing and smiles.)

NEBEKER: Your Honor, I think this must be the Wobbly silent defense and I think it merits a citation for contempt.
LANDIS: Contempt? Come on, Mr. Nebeker, we have 101 defendants, let's get someone up here and get on with it.
NEBEKER: Very well, Your Honor, thank you for sharing the contents of your mind ... I call Mr. Haywood for re-cross. ...

(Haywood doesn't hear.)

NEBEKER: I call Mr. Haywood for re-cross. ...

(Haywood takes the stand.)

NEBEKER: Mr. Haywood, let's talk about something very specific, the literature of the IWW. We have confiscated tons of your literature all over the country. Let's look at this copy of *Industrial Worker* ... now, here, where it says Meow at the head of this column, M-E-O-W, now that is intended to indicate the black sab-cat, the symbol of sabotage on the job, isn't it?
HAYWOOD: Well, some kind of cat anyhow.
NEBEKER: Well, what is the purpose of the black cat?
HAYWOOD: You know, if you saw a black cat go across your path, you would think you were gonna' have a little bad luck, if you were superstitious.

NEBEKER: If you were superstitious, huh? Don't you plaster this symbol all over fence posts and factory walls to terrorize employers into knuckling under to your demands?
VANDERVEER: I object.
LANDIS: Overruled.

(Haywood does not answer.)

NEBEKER: Let's look at this issue of *Solidarity*.... this article... dollar signs and Judge Landis... I assume this implies that Judge Landis is being bribed... did you see this before it was printed?
HAYWOOD: I don't think I've seen that, no.
NEBEKER: You know that this issue was found in IWW offices all over the country?
VANDERVEER: How could the witness know that, Mr. Nebeker?
NEBEKER: I don't know, how could he, Mr. Vanderveer... I thought as general secretary of the IWW it was his job to know what was going on... and I'm certain that he did but I doubt that this court will ever hear the truth about it from Mr. Haywood... Mr. Haywood, are you still a member of the Western Federation of Miners?
HAYWOOD: No.
NEBEKER: Weren't you thrown out of the Western Federation?
HAYWOOD: Yes, because of differences over....
NEBEKER: And weren't you thrown out of the Socialist Party?
HAYWOOD: Yes, we had disagreements over....
NEBEKER: So you were ejected from both these organizations because of your insistence on sabotage and disruption.
VANDERVEER: I object.
LANDIS: Overruled. Continue.
NEBEKER: Yes, fact, you have been thrown out of every labor organization you ever joined; in fact, Samuel Gompers, President of the American Federation of Labor, said you are a destructive, violent agitator who doesn't represent labor at all.
VANDERVEER: I object to this, Your Honor.
LANDIS: Overruled.
NEBEKER: Mr. Haywood, you pose as a labor leader, but by now we should all recognize that as a falsehood, you are King Haywood, are you not? King Haywood and his ambassadors of destruction?

(Motioning at Doran.)

HAYWOOD: *(Shrugs.)*

(Vanderver tries to interrupt, but is waved off by Landis.)

NEBEKER: You are a tyrannical sovereign, who sends his messengers across the country with orders to carry out strife and disorder, are you not?
HAYWOOD: What was that?
NEBEKER: Do you have a family, Mr. Haywood?
HAYWOOD: Yes.
NEBEKER: Are they in the court room?
HAYWOOD: No.
NEBEKER: Isn't it a fact that you have a crippled wife confined to a wheelchair and two young girls ... and that you abandoned them and have not seen them in years?
VANDERVEER: I object, Your Honor, this is character assassination....
LANDIS: Shut up, now this is pertinent....
NEBEKER: Well, Mr. Haywood, did you or did you not abandon your family?
HAYWOOD: I don't see them as much as I would like; I'm on the road a lot, but I continue to support them, in this society it's not unusual for working men to....
NEBEKER: Have you been supporting them from your prison salary for the last year? Did you support them while you were involved with the salon crowds of New York....
VANDERVEER: I object....
LANDIS: Shut up, Mr. Vanderveer.
NEBEKER: Ah ... maybe your wealthy women friends in Greenwich Village sent money to your family, is that the kind of support you are talking about?
HAYWOOD: No. I receive a salary from the IWW.
NEBEKER: Do you drink, Mr. Haywood?
HAYWOOD: I have on occasion, but my salary....
NEBEKER: On occasion? ... Come now ... you are a notorious drunkard....
VANDERVEER: I object....
LANDIS: One more outburst, Mr. Vanderveer, and you will be found in contempt and thrown out of this court room. Sit down, Mr. Vanderveer. Continue Mr. Nebeker.
NEBEKER: You don't believe in anything....
LANDIS: Sit down, Mr. Vanderveer.
NEBEKER: ... your country ... religious principles ... moral prin-

ciples ... the American way of life ... and you certainly don't represent labor ... just what do you represent? Now a real labor leader would have done what Mr. Gompers did, he mobilized labor in support of this war. ...

HAYWOOD: What was that?

NEBEKER: Patriotic labor unions like the A F of L whole-heartedly support this war, in fact Samuel Gompers has said the war is in the best interests of the labor movement.

(Haywood simply stares at Nebeker.)

NEBEKER: Finally, Mr. Haywood, perhaps you could answer the question which this trial was convened to answer. What is the IWW's position on the war, would you tell the jury exactly where the IWW stands on the war?

HAYWOOD: Mr. Nebeker, we have been through this all so many times before.

NEBEKER: Just answer the question.

DORAN: Yeah, Bill, tell him, tell him about the war.

HAYWOOD: I thought we had made it clear that the IWW—as an organization—has not taken a position on the war. Our individual members may ... haven't we been through this already?

NEBEKERS Mr. Haywood, we would like your position clarified, would you answer the question?

DORAN: The war, Bill, what about the draft, there were 98 casualties today ... only 98. ...

(Landis raps gavel, Vanderveer pulls Doran into his seat.)

NEBEKER: Mr. Haywood, are you going to answer my question? ... What was that, Mr. Haywood? ... Is this another silent defense? ... Your Honor, perhaps you could instruct the witness?

LANDIS: William. William!

NEBEKER: I'm finished with the witness, Your Honor ... I think that is sufficient, Your Honor, I have no one else to call.

LANDIS: Are we ready for summations?

VANDERVEER: Nothing has been proven here, and I will not present a final summation. This isn't a trial; it's a hanging!

LANDIS: Mr. Nebeker, do you have a summation?

NEBEKER: I most certainly do! These people and this organization have set themselves against the law. There is only one solution; they must be punished; they must be silenced so they cannot poison the minds of others. We can afford no leniency; it is not the function of this court to contemplate the reasons behind their acts. The acts are a violation of the law that was written specifically to stop this kind of activtity. We are not concerned with their motives or emotions; these things have no meaning. They have violated the espionage laws; they have aided the enemy; they have worked against the best interest of our society. A man has no right to revolution under the law. . . .

LANDIS: Well, that depends on how many men he can get to go in with him, in other words, whether he can put it over.

NEBEKER: Thank you, Your Honor . . . now . . . they are charged with having conspired to prevent by means of force the execution of laws. We say, that their use of the general strike was intended to cripple the basic industries and was intended to prevent this government from getting needed war materials . . . they wanted to extend the strike from the timber industry into the mines of the west, then into the mines of the middle west, then into Michigan, and then finally into the coal fields of Pennsylvania, evidence has been shown of that, then they wanted to extend it to the harvest fields, evidence has been shown of that. And finally when they were brazen in their confidence they would have shut down the entire transportation and shipping industry, railroads, teamsters, merchant marine, overseas trade. They would have destroyed the entire country. This government, which is all too slow to act, did finally wake up, found out what was going on and raided the headquarters of this outfit all over the country; it put a stop to the scheme that this trial has made absolutely apparent . . . and now you, the members of the jury . . . can put a final end to this plot by finding each and every defendant guilty on all charges.

LANDIS: Gentlemen of the jury, this is a conspiracy trial, and I will only instruct you on the meaning of conspiracy, in order to reach a verdict it is not necessary for you to find anyone guilty of committing a specific act . . . for the defendants are not charged with committing specific acts. The defendants are charged with conspiring to commit these acts, it does not matter if the acts were successful or even if they were attempted, you must only determine if they planned to commit them. And that is what your verdict must be based on. The jury will now withdraw and attempt to reach a verdict. . . .

(Jury exits. Narrator enters.)

NARRATOR: There were 40,000 pieces of evidence ... 505 counts against 101 defendants and the jury was out 55 minutes ... why, it would take that long just to read the batting order.

(Jury returns. Landis returns in robes.)

LANDIS: Have you reached a verdict?
JURY FOREMAN: Yes, we have, Your Honor.
LANDIS: The defendants will rise.
JURY FOREMAN: We find the defendants guilty on all charges. . . .
LANDIS: Having been found guilty by a jury of your peers ... I sentence you as follows: William D. Haywood ... twenty years ... Mr. Vanderveer, do you plan to appeal?
VANDERVEER: Yes, of course we'll appeal.
LANDIS: Then make that William D. Haywood, twenty years and 30,000 dollars fine; J. T. Doran, five years and 20,000 dollars fine.

(Landis continues to read sentences.)

NARRATOR: Well, that's the way it went ... when the Chicago White Sox threw the World Series in 1919, Kenesaw Mountain Landis finally reached the pinnacle of his career, he was named the first Commissioner of Baseball and told to clean up the league. Say it ain't so, Joe.

In June of '23 President Harding offered to commute the Wobblies' sentences if they would in no way encourage law breaking. They refused. . . .

Nebeker continued to prosecute for the Justice Department.

Vanderveer still continued to defend unpopular causes.

J. Edgar Hoover went on to plan the Palmer Raids and was eventually named the nation's top G Man.

Elizabeth Gurley Flynn continued as an organizer and finally became a Communist; only in America.

Red Doran served his five years in Leavenworth, as a Worker's Professor of Economics.

I saw Bill after he got out of Leavenworth on bail, between his ulcers and the diabetes and the booze he was a shadow of his former self, When the Supreme Court refused to hear the appeal, Bill, facing twenty years, skipped to the Soviet Union. He died a lonely, broken man a few years later.

And me ... *(Looking at his watch.)* I've got to see some reporters about a union.

(Exit, black out.)

A NOTE FROM THE PLAYWRIGHTS ON DOCUMENTARY SOURCES

We have combined straight documentary material from trial transcripts, speeches, newspapers, songs and poems with characters and situations we developed ourselves, and which may not have actually occurred. But we tried to capture some of the truth and all of the spirit of the people, events and times. For instance, the character of the Narrator was drawn from John Reed, Carl Sandburg, and Heywood Broun, reporters of the time. Needless to say, any one of these remarkable men could have stood alone.

We spoke to many Wobblies who lived through the events and would like to thank: Sam Dolgoff, Sophie Cohen, Minnie Corder, Oscar Sokol, Herbert Benjamin and Mrs. Pierce Wetter. We would also like to thank Fred Thompson, the I.W.W. historian in Chicago for his help and encouragement. Also special thanks to Len DeCaux for the basis for the Box Car Scene from his book, *Labor Radical*.

The project would not have been possible without the help of the staff of the Walter P. Reuther Archives of Labor History and Urban Affairs at Wayne State University and we would especially like to thank the staff of the Taminent Library at NYU.

We gathered enormous amounts of background information from many books, a partial listing of which includes: *The Autobiography of Big Bill Haywood; I Speak My Own Piece* by Elizabeth Gurley Flynn; *We Shall Be All* by Melvin Dubofsky; *Rebel Voices* by Joyce Kornbluh, *Big Bill Haywood and the Radical Labor Movement* by Joseph R. Conlin; *The Industrial Workers of the World: 1905-1917* by Philip S. Foner; *Aliens and Dissenters* by William Preston, Jr.; and *Opponents of War* by H. C. Peterson and Gilbert Fite.

The first production of *The Wobblies* was staged by the Labor Theater in 1976 under the direction of C. R. Portz.

STEWART BIRD has produced and directed several documentary films, including the award winning *Finally Got the News* which dealt with Detroit auto workers and *Coming Home* which dealt with Vietnam veterans. With Deborah Shaffer, he has just completed a film about the history of the Industrial Workers of the World which is also titled *The Wobblies* and should not be confused with the present play.

PETER T. ROBILOTTA has been a writer and an editor (*The Los Angeles Times* and Fairchild Publications), a free lance photographer, a commercial artist, and a theater tramp. He states that he has been a Wobbly ever since he first heard of the I.W.W.